Mindful Magic for The Kitchen Witch

CRAFTING NOURISHMENT AND SELF-CARE THROUGH RECIPES AND RITUALS

KELSEY PEARCE

Contents

Preface

This book is designed to offer a unique approach by blending the practices of kitchen witchery with modern mindfulness techniques to help you manage mental health and self-care. Magic is a powerful way to connect with yourself, find calm in chaos, and harness your inner strength.

However, it's essential to acknowledge that while the practices of a Kitchen Witch can provide valuable tools, they are not a substitute for professional mental health care. If you are struggling with severe anxiety, in crisis, or dealing with mental health challenges that feel beyond your control, seek help from a licensed therapist, counsellor, or healthcare provider. Your well-being is the top priority; professional support can provide the guidance and treatment you need.

This book is a companion on your journey to self-care, not a replacement for professional care when required. Use the practices and spells within these pages to complement the support you receive from professionals, and always remember that asking for help is a sign of strength.

Part I

Foundations of Kitchen Witchery for Mental Health

Chapter 1

WHAT IS A KITCHEN WITCH?

A Kitchen Witch is a transformative figure, blending the art of cooking with spiritual practices to turn everyday tasks in the kitchen into magical rituals. Instead of elaborate ceremonial magic, a Kitchen Witch focuses on the simple, mindful actions of preparing food, viewing the kitchen as a sacred space for nourishment and intention-setting. They believe that the energy and intention put into cooking can influence the mind, body, and spirit, infusing meals with personal meaning and purpose. Whether it's through the careful selection of ingredients, the way they stir a pot, or the mindful act of setting a table, a Kitchen Witch uses food and cooking to create connection, healing, and transformation.

In kitchen witchery, every herb, spice, and ingredient carries magical properties—rosemary for remembrance, garlic for protection, and honey for sweetness and harmony. The act of chopping, stirring, or even cleaning becomes a mindful ritual, creating space for spiritual practice in daily life. Kitchen Witches also use their craft to support others, often preparing food with specific intentions for love, healing, or community. By viewing the kitchen as the heart of the home and a place of creation, a Kitchen Witch weaves the sacred and mundane together, reminding us that magic is all around, especially in our shared meals.

For many of us, the kitchen is the heart of our home—a sacred space where nourishment, creativity, and connection intertwine. Whether we are cooking an elaborate meal in a state-of-the-art kitchen, experimenting with new recipes, or quickly nuking a frozen lasagna in the microwave, preparing food holds a special significance. It's a place where the aroma of spices fills the air, laughter and conversation flow, and memories are made over shared meals.

In today's fast-paced world, the kitchen often becomes a refuge, a place where we can ground ourselves amidst the chaos of daily life. Here, we can tap into our innate creativity, channeling our emotions into the ingredients we select and the dishes we create. This is the essence of kitchen witchery—a practice that combines the art of cooking with the magic of intention and mindfulness, offering a powerful means to nurture our mental health.

Kitchen witchery is not defined by the complexity of the meals we prepare or the tools we use. Witchcraft is rooted in the intention behind our actions. It invites us to embrace our unique cooking styles, whether whipping up a comforting stew from scratch or adding a sprinkle of love to a takeout dinner. This approach celebrates the beauty of inclusivity, acknowledging that each person's kitchen journey is valid and worthy of exploration.

This book will delve into the magical aspects of cooking, such as self-care and healing. We'll explore how the simple act of preparing food can serve as a ritual that nourishes our bodies, minds, and spirits. From infusing meals with the intention to using specific ingredients for their magical properties, you'll discover how kitchen witchery can empower you to create a space of comfort, healing, and joy.

Join us as we embark on this journey to discover the enchantment within your kitchen. Whether you are a seasoned cook, a novice in the kitchen, or someone who enjoys the occasional meal, this exploration of kitchen witchery will inspire you to harness the transformative power of food and cooking. Together, we will cultivate a practice that honours our unique paths, fosters mental well-being, and unites us with the nurturing spirit of the kitchen. Welcome to your magical culinary adventure!

Inclusivity in Kitchen Witchery—Magic for All

As our world and lives seem to rush toward chaos, modern witchcraft offers a counterbalance to the craziness. Rooted in intention and manifested with mindfulness, witchcraft facilitates a connection to our body, thoughts, beliefs, and more.

Various types of witchcraft exist, with different methods of practicing, but not all promote mental well-being. This book will focus on Kitchen Witchcraft with a caveat of inclusivity and harm-none.

Witches have long been a marginalized group, misunderstood and often pushed to the fringes of society to practice their craft. Today, witchcraft is a path that invites practitioners from all walks of life to embrace the diversity of identity, background, and personal beliefs. As a solo practitioner, you can define your magical journey, tailoring it to your unique needs and preferences without the constraints of tradition or dogma. Despite the existence of covens with specific guidelines or practices, there are abundant covens with diverse philosophies, enabling you to discover a group that resonates with your values if you extend your practice into a coven.

One of the greatest strengths of Kitchen Witchery is its accessibility. While there is often an emphasis on using whole, fresh, and seasonal ingredients, it's essential to recognize that the availability of food or tools should not define this practice. Not everyone has access to organic herbs, exotic spices, or gourmet ingredients, and that's perfectly fine. Kitchen Witchcraft is not limited to the elite food groups. Whether you're preparing a home-cooked meal from scratch or reheating chicken nuggets, the core of the practice lies in your intention and gratitude. Mindfully preparing the simplest meal can infuse it with the same energy and purpose as any elaborate dish.

In this book, we strive to provide balanced, adaptable, and inclusive guidance. The beauty of Kitchen Witchery is that it can be customized to your specific experience. You don't need expensive tools or rare ingredients to connect with the magic in your kitchen. A simple wooden spoon can become a wand, and a glass of tap water can hold as much symbolic power as a crystal chalice. By focusing on the energy you bring to your cooking, your gratitude for your ingredients, and your intentions for the meal, you transform even the simplest ingredients into a magical offering. This approach ensures that Kitchen Witchcraft is accessible to all, regardless of economic background, dietary restrictions, or living conditions. It's not the food that defines the magic, but the connection you create through your practice.

Ultimately, witchcraft, like mental health, is a deeply personal and evolving journey. There is no "one-size-fits-all" approach, and this book encourages you to honour your unique path. Whether you are a seasoned cook with a pantry full of fresh produce or someone making the most of what's on hand, Kitchen Witchery is about finding magic in the everyday moments of life, making your practice as individual as you are.

Ethical Considerations—Harm None

While some veins of witchcraft support hexes, curses, and ill will, that is not the purpose of this book. Harming others will eventually result in negative consequences for you. If you believe in the rule of three, whatever energy you put into the world will return to you threefold. With a practical lens, it is not good for our well-being to harm others, even if it feels justified. It will weigh on you. It is far better to focus on a positive intention to help you manage a difficult person or situation than to be intent to harm.

Other considerations include being mindful of cultural appropriation and ethical use of tools and resources.

Cultural Appropriation

Cultural appropriation can be a hard path to traverse. We may admire qualities that are part of a particular culture, ethnic, or spiritual group and want to incorporate those aspects into our practice. I would recommend the following when considering adopting aspects that may be cultural appropriation:

- Do you understand the significance of that practice item, symbol, music...?

- Are you being respectful about how you incorporate that practice item, symbol, music...into your practice?

- Will you profit from this action?

- Are you perpetuating stereotypes?

Even with the utmost intent to be respectful, we can offend. If that occurs, be willing to change and take the time to learn more about the significance of that practice to a culture.

An example of cultural appropriation risk is smudging. Smudging, especially with white sage, is a sacred ritual in many Native American and Indigenous cultures. It involves burning sacred herbs like sage, cedar, or sweetgrass to cleanse spaces and people of negative energy. It is now common to see the act of smudging used in witchcraft, yoga, and wellness circles. Practitioners of witchcraft should know the cultural significance. In addition, a witch should ensure the herbs are ethically sourced and respectful of the originating culture.

Another example is tarot cards. Now often used in witchcraft and divination, the original game and divination originated in Europe with the Romani. The Romani have been marginalized for most of history, and their cultural significance has been overlooked. Be mindful to acknowledge the cultural significance and not perpetuate harmful stereotypes.

Ethically Sourced Resources

Witchcraft is not immune from those seeking to profit from the practice. Like the example of the white sage in smudging, a witch should seek ethically sourced and renewable resources and avoid compromised resources for the pursuit of profit. As you will learn in this book, you can customize most spells and rituals using alternative products.

Not all products can be renewable or ethically sourced, and we may not be aware if it wasn't. We should aim to do our best.

Let's use an example to illustrate. If you needed lavender for a spell but the online resource you found seems a little sketchy, the other resource is outside your budget. What can you do? You could substitute the lavender with another herb that represents similar traits, like chamomile. You could use lavender oil. Another option could be to find an image or draw a flower to represent and use in a spell. There are some beautiful spells in which I have substituted a paper picture of an herb or flower and dissolved it in water. It just takes a little creativity and the focus of intent.

The Sacred Kitchen—The Heart of the Home

The kitchen has long been regarded as the heart of the home, a place where nourishment, warmth, and connection come together in perfect harmony. Whether it's a spacious, state-of-the-art kitchen with marble countertops and top-of-the-line appliances or a humble hot plate and mini fridge in a cozy dorm room, the magic of the kitchen transcends physical space. What makes a kitchen sacred isn't the size, luxury, or equipment; it's the energy you bring into it. It's the intention you stir into your meals, the memories you create, and the way you honour feeding yourself and others.

For a Kitchen Witch, the kitchen is a sanctuary. It's where we connect with our roots, ancestors, and deeper selves. Food is one of the most ancient forms of magic. From the moment early humans learned to cook over a fire, the kitchen has transformed—a space where raw ingredients are turned into something nourishing and sustaining. But this magic is not limited to professional chefs or those with access to gourmet ingredients. No matter the setup, the kitchen can become a sacred space, open to anyone willing to embrace its power.

What Makes a Kitchen Sacred?

A sacred kitchen isn't defined by perfection. You don't need artisanal spices or organic produce. You don't need to spend hours crafting a meal. What you need is mindfulness, love, and intention. In the same way that any tool or object can become magical through use, any kitchen space can become sacred through the energy you infuse into it. Here's how you can cultivate sacredness in your kitchen, no matter where you are:

Intention: It all begins with intention. Before you even pick up a knife or turn on the stove, take a moment to set your intention for the meal. Are you cooking for comfort, to uplift your mood, or to connect with loved ones? Even if you're making something simple, like a grilled cheese sandwich, focusing your thoughts on what you hope to achieve turns the act of cooking into a ritual. This makes the space around you feel magical, no matter how modest it may seem.

Connection: The kitchen is where we create connections—between ourselves and the food we eat, between those we cook for, and between our past and present. Cooking connects us to tradition, whether it's through family recipes passed down over generations or cultural dishes that remind us of home. When you prepare food, you are participating in the same rituals that countless people have engaged in—turning ingredients into something that sustains the body and spirit.

Creativity and Adaptability: Cooking is inherently creative, even when you're making something as simple as ramen noodles in a dorm. It's about improvisation, using what you have on hand, and embracing the outcome. When we look at cooking as a form of alchemy, every meal becomes a small magic act. Kitchen Witchery teaches us to see every meal as an opportunity to create something special, no matter the ingredients or circumstances.

Mindfulness: Cooking can be a meditation. When you chop vegetables, stir a pot, or knead dough, you ground yourself in the present moment. Repeating these tasks allows your mind to focus, your body to relax, and your spirit to connect with the task at hand. In Kitchen Witchery, these seemingly mundane tasks are elevated into sacred actions. Whether you're brewing tea or simmering soup, the focus and care you put into the process imbues the space with positive energy.

A Kitchen for Everyone

Your kitchen doesn't need to look like the pages of a glossy magazine to be sacred. There is no need for fancy equipment or dishes you would be heartbroken to break. In truth, you don't even need a room labelled "kitchen". Outdoor cooking, like camping or road trips and cooler meals, could be the stage for a kitchen witch. Likewise, temporary accommodations such as a hotel room could become your kitchen.

Personalize Your Space: Make your kitchen yours, even if it's a small corner or a shared space. Add small touches that bring you joy and inspire your creativity—a favourite dish towel, a sprig of herbs by the window or a candle that you light before cooking. These small touches make the space feel personal, grounding you in your magical practice. This can be leveraged even when travelling. I brought a travel mug with llamas, a gift from my children, while on business travel. My ritual involved selecting hotel-offered teas, and while the tea infused, I thought of how much love I had for my children despite being away; I focused on their safety. In a way, the travel mug became a magical chalice in my intention to manifest safety for my kids.

Create a Ritual: Before cooking, take a moment to cleanse your space. It could be as simple as wiping down the counters, lighting a small candle, or saying a quiet blessing over the ingredients you're about to use. This intentionality shifts the space's energy, helping you feel centred and connected to the moment.

Focus on Gratitude: Every time you step into your kitchen, pause to feel gratitude. Gratitude for your food, the ability to prepare it, and the opportunity to nourish yourself and others. This small shift in mindset transforms the act of cooking into an act of devotion. Whether preparing a feast or heating up leftovers, gratitude elevates the experience.

Respect the Ingredients: Treat each ingredient as if it were special, because it is. Treat them with care even if you're using simple, inexpensive items. When you respect the ingredients, you respect the Earth and the energy that goes into growing, harvesting, and preparing them. This respect transforms even the most straightforward meal into something sacred.

The Magic of Cooking

Cooking is, at its heart, a kind of everyday magic. We gather raw ingredients—flour, water, spices, maybe a bit of butter—and follow a series of steps, often ending up with something completely different and infinitely more delicious than what we started with. Science might explain this transformation, but watching a pot of soup go from a hodgepodge of veggies and broth to a rich, soul-warming dish or seeing bread dough double in size as if by enchantment feels undeniably magical. After all, who hasn't been a little mesmerized by watching dough rise, or slightly amazed at the way eggs, flour, and sugar morph into a fluffy cake?

And let's be real: even if there's a scientific reason for everything, some parts of cooking just seem a little like wizardry. Take yeast, for example. Sprinkle a bit of it into warm water with a spoonful of sugar, and it practically springs to life, bubbling and foaming as it prepares to work its alchemical wonders on your bread dough. Or think about caramelizing onions: they go from sharp and pungent to sweet, dark, and velvety after a little heat and patience. Sure, we know why it happens, but knowing the science behind it doesn't make it any less magical to witness.

What elevates this process into kitchen witchery is the intention behind it. When you stir a sauce with a focus on love or add herbs with a specific hope or desire in mind, you're infusing that meal with a little extra something—your own energy, your wishes, your care. The meal becomes more than a set of steps followed to an edible end; it's a ritual, a small spell you're casting with every pinch of salt or drizzle of olive oil. This focus, this connection to the ingredients and process, is what truly brings the magic of cooking to life for a kitchen witch. Because at the end of the day, cooking may be science, but it's also transformation, connection, and a dash of magic we can share.

Magic in Every Meal?

For a Kitchen Witch, there's no hierarchy in cooking. A five-course meal and a quick snack can hold the same magical energy if made with intention, mindfulness, and love. This is the true power of the sacred kitchen—it's not about what you have but what you bring to it. Your space, however modest, becomes a portal for transformation and connection. It becomes a space where you can nurture yourself and those you love, offering nourishment for the body, heart, and soul.

But realistically, you don't have to make every meal a ritual. I would find that exhausting, and it would lose its significance for me. Intentional or mindful sacred cooking moments can be created, but they are not obligatory for every meal. You need to trust your instincts and develop your practice.

As a parent, I find it stressful to ensure that meals are prepared that hit all or at least most of the food groups every day. I would not want to add to the stress of following rituals each time. I have found that in moments of craziness, I appreciate a simple cooking act, like making toast. It can engage all of my senses, and I can visualize my intention. When there is calmness in my life, the larger meals or cooking with a child is a time for a little extra magic.

Does a Kitchen Witch Have to be a Great Cook?

A Kitchen Witch doesn't have to be a superb cook—what matters is the intention behind the meal, not perfection. Kitchen Witchery is about infusing love, mindfulness, and magic into preparing food, whether making an elaborate feast or heating frozen pizza. When a recipe flops, it's simply part of the process, much like life's trials. The beauty of kitchen magic is that it embraces imperfection, teaching us to be patient, adaptable, and kind to ourselves. Even when a dish doesn't turn out as expected, the energy you put into it still holds power. You can take a moment to reflect on what went wrong, laugh it off, and focus on the intention you had. After all, the effort and care you give that matter most in Kitchen Witchery, not culinary mastery.

Is this a Cookbook?

While there will be recipes, this is not a cookbook. Rather, it is a reference book for spell crafting intended to support mental health. The focus will be on spell crafting in the kitchen, from set-up to prep, eating, and cleaning up.

Like other spell crafting, you can personalize recipes to support your taste, food restrictions, and ingredient availability. This book is not restricted to one type of food, nor will it always present the 'healthiest' suggestion.

Chapter 2

CREATING A SACRED KITCHEN SPACE

A sacred kitchen space is not defined by luxury or extravagance—it's about cultivating a space where magic, intention, and nourishment come together. Whether you have a gourmet kitchen, a tiny counter in a shared apartment, or a temporary setup in a hotel room, you can create a sacred kitchen that reflects your values, energy, and personal journey. The kitchen is where transformation happens, both in the food you prepare and in the energy you bring to the space. This chapter will guide you in crafting a sacred kitchen space, no matter where life takes you, by setting up altars, using meaningful objects, and practicing intentional cleansing and organizing.

Setting Up Your Kitchen Altar

A kitchen altar is a small, intentional space where you place items that hold meaning, inspire creativity, or remind you of your connection to the sacred. For some, this might include traditional magical tools like crystals, herbs, or candles. For others, it could be something as simple as a favourite coffee mug, a wooden spoon passed down from a loved one, or a mismatched bowl that has become a cherished symbol of resilience. The beauty of kitchen witchcraft is that there is no right or wrong way to set up an altar—what matters is that it holds personal significance to you.

Using Crystals

Crystals are commonly used in witchcraft for their energetic properties, and they can be a wonderful addition to your kitchen space. For example, you might place a piece of clear quartz to amplify your intentions, a small chunk of rose quartz to bring love and warmth into your cooking, or a slice of citrine to invite abundance into your life. However, the most essential aspect of your kitchen altar isn't the objects themselves, but the meaning behind them.

Crystals and Methods to Incorporate

Family Meals—Rose Quartz

Symbolism: Love, harmony, and connection.

Cooking Intention: When preparing a meal meant to bring the family together or foster a sense of love and unity, Rose Quartz is the perfect crystal to have nearby. It symbolizes unconditional love and strengthens bonds, making it ideal for family dinners, gatherings, or celebrations. Place a piece of Rose Quartz in your kitchen or on your table to encourage warmth, understanding, and harmony among loved ones.

Amethyst—Healing Meals

Symbolism: Healing, peace, and spiritual protection.

Cooking Intention: Amethyst is a powerful crystal for emotional and physical healing, making it ideal when preparing nourishing meals for someone who is sick, recovering, or in need of extra comfort. Its soothing energy can enhance the healing power of soups, teas, or broths made to soothe cold or flu symptoms. Keep an Amethyst nearby as you brew healing teas or cook comforting meals, and focus on infusing your food with peace and recovery.

Smoky Quartz—Grief and Comfort

Symbolism: Grounding, release, and emotional healing.

Cooking Intention: When cooking for someone grieving, Smoky Quartz is a wonderful crystal that supports the process of release and transformation. It helps ground emotional pain and gently assists in letting go of sorrow. This makes it a perfect companion when preparing comforting, simple meals meant to bring solace during times of loss. You might keep Smoky Quartz on your altar or beside the stove as you bake or prepare soothing dishes, such as casseroles or stews.

Citrine—Cooking for Prosperity or Success

Symbolism: Abundance, prosperity, and creativity.

Cooking Intention: Citrine is known for its energy of abundance and success, making it a wonderful crystal to use when cooking for prosperity. If you're preparing a meal to manifest financial abundance or to celebrate a new venture, consider keeping Citrine close. Whether you're preparing a meal to bring prosperity into your home or sharing food to celebrate a personal victory, Citrine encourages optimism, joy, and creativity in the kitchen.

Clear Quartz—Nourishing the Soul

Symbolism: Clarity, amplification, and spiritual nourishment.

Cooking Intention: Clear Quartz is a versatile crystal that amplifies intentions and can be used in almost any cooking scenario. It's particularly effective when preparing a meal with the goal of nourishing both body and soul. If you're focusing on spiritual or emotional well-being—perhaps making a meal to share mindful moments, meditate, or create balance—Clear Quartz can help channel that energy. Place it nearby to amplify the love and healing you want to infuse into your dishes.

Black Tourmaline—Grounding and Stability

Symbolism: Protection, grounding, and stability.

Cooking Intention: Black Tourmaline is excellent for grounding and protection, making it ideal when you're cooking a meal that's meant to bring a sense of security, stability, or calm in stressful times. When making comfort foods like stews, root vegetables, or hearty breads, having Black Tourmaline nearby can help keep you grounded and centred. It's perfect for meals cooked to ease stress or protect against negative energy.

Carnelian—Creative Cooking

Symbolism: Creativity, vitality, and motivation.

Cooking Intention: Carnelian is the crystal of creativity and vitality, perfect for when you're experimenting in the kitchen or looking for inspiration. Whether you're trying a new recipe, making something for a special occasion, or infusing your food with excitement and passion, Carnelian will enhance your creative energy. It's great to keep in your kitchen when you want to spice things up—literally and figuratively!

Garnet—Cooking with Intention for Romance

Symbolism: Passion, love, and vitality.

Cooking Intention: If you're preparing a meal with the intention of kindling romance or deepening a passionate connection, Garnet is the crystal for you. It is linked to love, attraction, and the warmth of affection, making it an ideal companion when cooking for a romantic evening or a date night. Whether it's a sensual dessert or a comforting meal for two, keep Garnet nearby to amplify love and connection.

Working with Crystals in the Kitchen: A Safe Approach

Some practitioners may feel drawn to the idea of placing crystals directly in their drinks or food, but it's important to understand that this practice can come with risks. Many crystals contain elements like copper, lead, or other minerals that can leach into liquids, potentially causing health issues. Additionally, some crystals are water-soluble or fragile, meaning they can erode or break down when exposed to moisture, ruining both the crystal and the drink.

Instead of placing crystals directly in food or drink, I recommend a safer approach: keeping crystals nearby to infuse your kitchen and food preparation areas with their energy. You can place crystals around your kitchen altar, next to your stove, or near your food as you cook. For example, you might keep a piece of amethyst beside your teapot to channel healing energy into the tea or place a rose quartz on the dining table to promote love and harmony during meals. This way, you can still benefit from the crystals' energies without risking any unintended health effects or damaging the stones themselves.

The Vegetable Crisper in the Fridge

For adding energy to your vegetable crisper while being mindful of humidity, clear quartz. Clear quartz is known for its amplifying properties, enhancing the natural energy of the vegetables and promoting freshness. Its durability makes it safe for environments with fluctuating temperatures and humidity, like the fridge.

Another good option is green aventurine. Known for its association with abundance, vitality, and growth, green aventurine aligns beautifully with the fresh energy of vegetables. Like quartz, it can handle humidity, so it's a resilient addition to your crisper drawer.

You could also add the crystals to a pantry or spice cupboard. Just be sure to periodically cleanse and recharge the stones outside of the fridge, as they'll benefit from a refresh after being stored in a cool, enclosed space.

By using crystals in this way, you can honour the magical properties of these natural elements while also prioritizing safety and well-being.

Meaningful Objects

Imagine you have salt and pepper shakers that once belonged to a grandparent. To someone else, they may seem like ordinary kitchen items, but for you, they carry the energy of love, family, and connection. Whenever you season a meal with those shakers, you're not just adding flavour—you're honouring your family and the memories shared around the table.

Mismatched Dishes:

Over time, it is common to be left with a few dishes that do not match a set. While they can be donated if you prefer matching dishes, those survivors can also hold representation value. You could see it as a symbol of perseverance and strength, or it could invoke specific memories that add value to your ritual. The following are examples of how a dish can become part of your symbolic imagery in spell crafting and kitchen witchcraft.

The Lone Bowl: After surviving countless meals and near misses, you have one bowl left from a set. This bowl could represent strength and perseverance. You could use it as the soup bowl for treating colds. You build the intention to pass strength from the bowl to the unwell person. It is all about perspective.

The Little Spoon: As children, my cousins and I raced to get the little brass-coloured spoon at my grandmother's cottage. My daughter also has a favourite little spoon that came from the same mismatch set at my grandmother's. That spoon symbolizes childhood joy for the simple things, like the design of a spoon. I love seeing my daughter's face when the table is set with her special spoon.

Practical Tips for Small, Shared, or Transient Spaces

For many people, creating a sacred kitchen space isn't about having an entire room to dedicate to magic—it's about making the most of what you have. If you live in a small apartment, share a kitchen with roommates, or find yourself moving frequently, you can still create meaningful, sacred spaces.

In shared spaces, it's important to be mindful of others while still honouring your practice. Consider keeping your most treasured items—like a crystal, a special spoon, or a small candle—stored in a personal drawer or box when not in use. This not only protects your items from damage but also allows you to maintain your sacred space without infringing on communal areas. When appropriate, you can even share with your roommates why certain objects hold significance to you. For example, explaining that a particular mug belonged to a beloved family member can foster understanding and respect for your magical practice.

If you find yourself in a transient situation, such as staying in a hotel, a dorm room, or on a camping trip, you can still bring a sense of sacredness to your cooking space. In a hotel room, a travel altar might consist of a small candle, a pocket-sized crystal, and a simple cloth to lay your items on. Even in a camping setting, you can create magic by cooking over a fire, connecting to nature, and using a favourite travel cup to enjoy your meal with intention. It's not the space itself that matters—it's the energy and intention you bring to it.

Cleansing and Organizing Your Space

A cluttered kitchen can lead to a cluttered mind, and one of the simplest ways to create a sacred kitchen space is through the ritual of cleaning and organizing. Just as decluttering your physical space can bring mental clarity, cleansing your kitchen can clear away stagnant or negative energy, making room for magic to flow freely.

The Ritual of Decluttering

Start by decluttering your kitchen space. This doesn't need to be a massive overhaul; it can be as simple as going through your cupboards and removing expired items, reorganizing your spices, or clearing off your countertops. Decluttering allows you to clear both physical and mental space, creating a more intentional environment for your magical work. As you declutter, reflect on what no longer serves you—both in your kitchen and in your life. Just as you release an old, chipped plate, you can mentally release habits, thoughts, or patterns that no longer align with your well-being.

When you release what no longer serves you, you allow new, positive energy to enter. For instance, while organizing your pantry, you may decide to keep only the ingredients that bring you joy or that align with your health goals. Even a small shift like this can feel like magic, allowing you to connect with your food and your space in a deeper, more meaningful way.

Infusing Cleaning with Intention

Cleansing your kitchen is more than just wiping down surfaces—it's an opportunity to infuse your space with positive energy. You can make this as simple or as elaborate as you like. If you enjoy using essential oils, you might create a homemade cleaning spray using water, vinegar, and a few drops of lemon or lavender oil, each chosen for their magical and cleansing properties. Lemon, for instance, is known for its ability to clear negative energy, while lavender brings a sense of peace and calm.

Alternatively, if you prefer simplicity, a clean cloth and a bit of soap can be just as powerful. The key is to focus on your intentions while you clean. As you wipe down your counters, imagine that you're wiping away stress, anxiety, or negativity. As you sweep the floor, picture yourself sweeping out any lingering doubts or fears. When your space is clean, it will feel lighter, brighter, and ready for the magic you're about to create.

Even in transient or temporary spaces, cleansing and organizing can have a profound impact. If you're staying in a hotel, for example, take a moment to wipe down the kitchenette or arrange your cooking tools with care. By making small adjustments to the space, you can claim it as your own, even if only for a short time.

Bringing the Sacred Into Everyday Spaces

The sacred kitchen isn't about having a perfect, Pinterest-worthy setup. It's about creating a space where you feel connected to your magic, no matter what form that takes. Whether you're in a fully equipped kitchen or working with a hot plate and mini fridge, you can make any space sacred by infusing it with intention, care, and a bit of creativity.

Imagine you're a college student living in a dorm room with nothing but a microwave and a mini-fridge. Even in this modest setup, you can create magic. Your sacred space might include a favourite mug, a crystal placed on top of your fridge, and a simple ritual of saying a blessing over your food before you eat. Or, perhaps you're living out of a suitcase in a hotel room. By lighting a small, travel-sized candle and mindfully preparing a cup of tea, you're turning an otherwise sterile environment into a space of warmth and reflection.

The Power of Intention and the Sacred Space

The sacred kitchen isn't defined by the size of your space or the tools at your disposal—it's created through the energy you bring to it. Whether you're simmering a pot of soup in a family home or making ramen noodles in a tiny apartment, your kitchen becomes sacred when you approach it with intention, love, and gratitude. As you cleanse, organize, and set up your kitchen altar, remember that every item, every action, and every meal holds the potential for magic. Your kitchen is the heart of your home, and with a little care, it can become the heart of your spiritual practice as well.

Chapter 3

CRAFTING YOUR KITCHEN BOOK OF SHADOWS

T his is probably one of my favourite topics. I loved the TV series Charmed, the 1998 version, not that there was anything wrong with the most recent version. I had the complete DVD collection of Charmed that looked like the Book of Shadows. How I wish it had been real.

Now, I don't have the same skill as the artists from the TV series, but it didn't mean I could not have more own Book of Shadows or Grimoire if you prefer.

A Book of Shadows is not a journal. For many, the idea of journaling conjures images of neatly penned lines filling the pages of a pristine notebook, a task often laden with expectations and the pressure to articulate thoughts perfectly. If you're like me and the thought of traditional journaling sends you into a spiral of frustration and resistance, fear not! This chapter will guide you in creating a Kitchen Book of Shadows that aligns with your unique style and embraces the magic of your culinary journey without the constraints of conventional journaling.

Understanding the Kitchen Book of Shadows

In the realm of kitchen witchery, a Book of Shadows serves as a personal grimoire, a sacred space where you can document your experiences, recipes, and magical insights. Unlike a traditional journal, your Kitchen Book of Shadows can be as messy, colourful, and eclectic as you are. It's not about neatness or structure; it's about capturing the essence of your culinary magic and connecting with your intentions in a way that feels authentic to you. Unlike traditional journals, your Book of Shadows is a reference you can go back to repeatedly.

Organizing Your Kitchen Book of Shadows

You don't need to follow a strict structure when organizing your Kitchen Book of Shadows. Instead, let your intuition guide you. Here are some ideas to create a personalized system that resonates with your style:

Sections by Theme: Consider dividing your book into sections based on themes that inspire you. For example, you might have a section for seasonal recipes, another for herbal magic, and one for special occasions. This allows you to easily navigate your culinary creations while infusing each section with the energy of its theme.

Recipe and Ritual Pairings: Pair your favourite recipes with corresponding rituals or magical practices. For example, if you have a recipe for a nourishing broth, include a note about the ingredients' protection and grounding properties. This creates a holistic approach, reminding you of the magic behind each dish.

Loose Pages and Flexibility: Instead of feeling constrained by bound pages, consider using a binder or scrapbook format that allows for loose pages. This way, you can easily add, remove, or rearrange entries as your culinary journey evolves. Embrace the messiness and fluidity of your practice, allowing it to grow and change with you.

Consider going paperless: Create a folder in a cloud-based application to save links, experiences, and pictures. Ensure you tag items with useful words to help you locate them again. Another option is to email yourself with the same content; if you have children, you could create a unique email address that you can pass to them in the future that has all of your notes, thoughts, images...There is nothing that says a book of shadows has to be an ancient-looking tome.

Embracing Your Style

Visual Inspiration: If writing feels daunting, consider using visual elements to express your thoughts and experiences. Create collages from magazine cutouts, photos, or drawings that inspire you. Through imagery, capture the essence of your cooking adventures, allowing your creativity to flow freely without the confines of words.

Doodles and Sketches: Your Kitchen Book of Shadows can be adorned with doodles, sketches, or playful drawings that reflect your culinary journey. Don't worry about artistic perfection; simply allow your hand to move and capture the essence of your thoughts and feelings. You might sketch the herbs you use, the dishes you create, or even the energy you wish to invoke.

Recipe Cards: Create a collection of recipe cards that embody your favourite dishes, each adorned with magical notes, intentions, or personal anecdotes. You can mix handwritten cards with printed ones, using colourful pens or markers to add flair. This tactile approach allows you to engage with your cooking process in an enjoyable and meaningful way.

Use A Creative Application: An application like Canva, even the free version, will allow you to create eclectic mashups of graphics and text in different fonts, upload images, add pages...There are so many options. Save them as a PDF and download or print. If you want to change something, just go back and edit the page. The "Warm Our Hearts Hot Chocolate" was created in Canva and uses only free options only. It may take a little more digging to find the right free graphic but the creative reward is worth the effort. This recipe was also done on a grey scale to complement the book.

Capturing Magical Intentions

Your Kitchen Book of Shadows is the perfect place to document your intentions and the magical properties of the ingredients you use. Here's how to approach this aspect without the pressure of traditional journaling:

Ingredient Notes: Rather than writing lengthy paragraphs, jot down short notes or keywords associated with the magical properties of herbs and ingredients. For example, next to the entry for rosemary, you might write "remembrance," "clarity," or "protection." Feel free to use symbols or drawings that resonate with you, creating a visual language that enhances your connection to the ingredients.

WARM OUR HEARTS
Hot Chocolate

- 4c Milk (any kind)
- 1/4c unsweetened cocoa powder
- 1/4c sugar
- 1/2 tsp vanilla extract
- pinch of salt
- Optional toppings

Combine in microwave safe bowl. Microwave for 4 minutes checking every minute and stirring.
Divide into 4 servings and add toppings!

Use Grama's Cup

- Don't let it boil over!
- Add 1/4c chocolate chips for richer hot chocolate
- Stir clockwise for connection

Meal Intentions: Before you prepare a meal, take a moment to think about the energy you wish to infuse into your dish. Instead of writing a formal intention, consider using a simple phrase or mantra that captures your desire. Write this phrase on the page where you document the recipe, and let it serve as a guiding force while you cook.

Reflections on Experiences: After cooking, take a moment to reflect on how the meal turned out, how it made you feel, and any insights you gained from the experience. Instead of writing a formal summary, allow yourself to jot down quick bullet points or phrases that capture your emotions and thoughts. You might simply write, "Felt grounded after the nourishing soup" or "The chocolate cake brought joy."

Making It a Living Document

Your Kitchen Book of Shadows is a living document that reflects your growth and evolution as a kitchen witch. It's a space where you can explore, experiment, and celebrate your culinary adventures without the burden of perfection. Here are some ways to keep it vibrant and engaging:

Add Photos: Capture moments from your cooking experiences by adding photos to your Kitchen Book of Shadows. Snap pictures of your beautifully plated dishes, the ingredients you've gathered, or the gatherings with loved ones. These visuals will add depth and warmth to your book.

Incorporate Nature: Consider pressing leaves, flowers, or herbs into your pages. This can create a sensory experience and serve as a reminder of the natural elements that inspire your cooking. Each pressed item holds its own magic, enhancing your connection to the ingredients.

Encourage Collaboration: Invite friends or family members to contribute to your Kitchen Book of Shadows. They can add their favourite recipes, insights, or experiences, creating a collaborative space filled with diverse perspectives and flavors.

Take Your Kitchen Book of Shadows to the Next Level

Now that we've established the foundation of your Kitchen Book of Shadows, let's delve deeper into its potential. This section will explore additional elements that can enhance your experience, foster creativity, and provide a deeper connection to your kitchen witchery practice.

Documenting Culinary Experiments

Your Kitchen Book of Shadows is a wonderful place to document your culinary experiments—those playful attempts to create something new or to modify existing recipes. Here are some ideas for capturing these adventures:

Successes and Failures: Don't shy away from documenting both your successes and failures. Include notes on what worked well, what didn't, and any adjustments you would make next time. This practice encourages growth and creativity, reminding you that experimentation is a vital part of the culinary journey.

Flavour Pairing Trials: Experiment with unusual flavor pairings and document the results. For instance, if you combine unexpected ingredients, note how they interacted and what flavors emerged. This exploration can spark new ideas and encourage boldness in your cooking.

Themed Cooking Nights: Host themed cooking nights where you explore a particular cuisine or ingredient. Document the recipes you tried, your thoughts on the experience, and any magical intentions you set for the evening. This can serve as inspiration for future gatherings.

Infusing Personal Stories and Memories

Your Kitchen Book of Shadows can become a tapestry of personal stories and memories woven together with your culinary experiences. Here's how to add this layer of richness to your book:

Family Recipes and Ancestral Connections: Include cherished family recipes that have been passed down through generations. Document the stories behind these recipes, who they came from, and what they mean to you. This adds depth and connection to your culinary heritage.

Cooking with Loved Ones: Capture moments spent cooking with friends or family. Document the laughter, conversations, and insights shared during those times. You might even include photographs or mementos from these gatherings to enhance the narrative.

Food as Memory Trigger: Reflect on how certain dishes evoke memories or emotions. When you document recipes, consider including a brief note about the memories they conjure or the feelings they inspire. This connection can transform your cooking into a more profound experience.

Integrating Mindful Eating Practices

The act of cooking is only one part of the culinary experience; mindful eating is equally important. Incorporate this aspect into your Kitchen Book of Shadows:

Mindful Eating Reflections: After enjoying a meal, take a moment to reflect on the experience. How did the flavors make you feel? What emotions did the meal evoke? Write down your reflections to cultivate a deeper appreciation for your culinary creations.

Setting the Table: Document your table-setting rituals and how they enhance the dining experience. Consider the energy you wish to create with your table decor, such as using candles, flowers, or crystals. Capture your thoughts on how these elements contribute to the overall atmosphere.

Gratitude Practices: Create a section dedicated to gratitude practices related to food. Document the ways you express gratitude before and after meals, whether through spoken words, written notes, or even small rituals. This practice fosters a sense of appreciation and connection to the nourishment you receive.

Your Kitchen Book of Shadows Reflects You

As you continue to develop your Kitchen Book of Shadows, remember that it is a reflection of your unique journey as a kitchen witch. There's no right or wrong way to express yourself in this space—what matters most is that you find joy, creativity, and connection throughout the process.

This book is a living testament to your culinary adventures, a sacred space where the magic of your cooking can flourish. Embrace the spontaneity, the messiness, and the beauty of your experiences as you craft a personal tome that captures the essence of your kitchen witchery. May your Kitchen Book of Shadows serve as a source of inspiration, empowerment, and a celebration of the magic that exists within every meal you create!

Chapter 4

MAGICAL INGREDIENTS

Fruits and Vegetables:

Fruits and vegetables offer a wealth of symbolism, energy, and natural properties that a Kitchen Witch can incorporate into spellcraft, adding layers of meaning and magic to everyday cooking. By choosing specific fruits and vegetables for their symbolic and energetic properties, you can align your meals with particular intentions, whether for love, healing, protection, or abundance. Here are some common fruits and vegetables and how they can be used in spells and rituals:

Apples—Love, Wisdom, and Healing

Properties: Often associated with love and romance, apples are symbols of beauty, wisdom, and abundance.

Spellcraft Ideas: Use apples in love spells by baking them into pies or desserts with an intention for harmony or attraction. Cutting an apple horizontally reveals a five-pointed star, which represents protection and balance, making it perfect for spells seeking harmony in relationships or self-love.

Garlic—Protection and Purification

Properties: Garlic has strong protective qualities and is traditionally used to ward off negativity.

Spellcraft Ideas: Hang garlic in your kitchen or add it to dishes to create a protective energy in your space. You can also incorporate garlic in cleansing spells to purify both food and the surrounding energy. Roasting garlic cloves and spreading them in a meal can serve as a ritual for inner strength and resilience.

Lemons—Cleansing, Purification, and Positivity

Properties: Lemons are associated with purification, cleansing, and lifting spirits. They are often used to remove negativity.

Spellcraft Ideas: Lemon juice can be added to teas, broths, or water for spells focused on clearing emotional blockages or starting fresh. Lemon zest in baking or cooking infuses food with positive energy and mental clarity. A simple ritual might involve squeezing fresh lemon into the water while focusing on releasing negativity and inviting positivity.

Onions—Protection and Layered Healing

Properties: Onions have strong protective qualities and are associated with resilience and healing on multiple levels.

Spellcraft Ideas: The layers of an onion can symbolize different facets of healing, making it powerful in spells aimed at addressing complex emotional or physical wounds. You can incorporate onions into soups or stews with the intention of shedding negative energies or unwanted influences layer by layer.

Potatoes—Grounding, Stability, and Nourishment

Properties: Potatoes, as root vegetables, are strongly connected to grounding and stability.

Spellcraft Ideas: Use potatoes in dishes where grounding and strengthening energy are needed, such as comforting meals for family or when you're feeling unsettled. Mashing potatoes with intention can be a mindful ritual to infuse your meal with feelings of security, calm, and rootedness.

Tomatoes—Love, Passion, and Protection

Properties: Often linked to love and passion, tomatoes are also associated with protection, particularly in relationships.

Spellcraft Ideas: Use tomatoes in sauces, salads, or soups to amplify love and passion or to protect relationships. For a love ritual, make a tomato sauce while focusing on deepening bonds or reigniting romance. The bright red colour makes tomatoes ideal for spells focused on vitality, courage, and heart-centred intentions.

Carrots—Success, Luck, and Fertility

Properties: Carrots symbolize success, good fortune, and fertility, associated with their connection to the earth and vibrant orange colour.

Spellcraft Ideas: Roast or cook carrots with an intention for prosperity or success in new ventures. Carrots can be included in meals made for friends or loved ones as a way of sharing blessings and abundance. If fertility or new beginnings are part of your intention, carrots make a great addition to spells and dishes aligned with growth.

Pumpkin and Squash—Abundance and Prosperity

Properties: Pumpkins and other squashes are symbols of abundance, prosperity, and generosity.

Spellcraft Ideas: When cooking with pumpkin or squash, focus on abundance, especially around harvest times. Bake pumpkin bread or make soups as part of prosperity rituals, visualizing the wealth you wish to attract. Their seeds can also be dried and kept as symbols of growth or carried as charms for good fortune.

Peppers—Energy, Courage, and Transformation

Properties: Peppers, with their spicy flavour, are linked to courage, energy, and transformation.

Spellcraft Ideas: Use peppers in spells and dishes where you want to create movement, change, or energize yourself. Adding chilli peppers to food to boost courage can be especially empowering before taking on challenges. If you're working on a project or personal goal, cooking with peppers can help instil the energy to persevere.

Bananas—Joy, Fertility, and Attraction

Properties: Bananas are associated with happiness, attraction, and fertility.

Spellcraft Ideas: Add bananas to smoothies or desserts as part of spells for happiness and attraction. They're particularly useful for building confidence and joy in self-love rituals. Place a banana on your altar or use it as a base for a sweet treat to boost positivity and light-hearted energy.

Ginger—Strength, Healing, and Luck

Properties: Ginger is known for its warming, invigorating qualities and is used in spells for strength, health, and protection.

Spellcraft Ideas: Incorporate ginger into teas or meals to encourage resilience, especially during emotional or physical fatigue. The spicy flavour of ginger can boost courage or warm relationships. Make ginger tea intending to heal, or use it in baking to bring strength and protection into your home.

Celery—Psychic Awareness and Balance

Properties: Celery is linked to intuition, focus, and balance.

Spellcraft Ideas: Use celery in soups or juices when seeking clarity, focus, or psychic awareness. It's great for spells that enhance mindfulness or intuition, helping to ground your spiritual insights. Celery stalks are often bundled, symbolizing connection and unity, making them ideal for meals shared with others to encourage understanding.

As we will see in later chapters, combining ingredients based on magical properties

A Kitchen Witch can create meals that align with their goals and intentions by thoughtfully selecting fruits and vegetables for their symbolic properties. Remember, it's not the ingredient itself that carries the magic but the focus and intention you bring to the preparation. Whether you're cooking for love, healing, protection, or abundance, the ingredients in your kitchen can be powerful allies in your spellcraft.

Other Household Staples:

Aside from fruits and vegetables, many other foods have magical properties that have been revered in kitchen witchery and folk traditions. These ingredients are often staples in everyday cooking and carry unique energies that can align with specific intentions. Here are some examples of common foods with magical significance:

Eggs—Fertility, New Beginnings, and Transformation

Magical Properties: Eggs symbolize fertility, rebirth, and potential. They represent the cycle of life and are used in spells for new beginnings, growth, and protection. In some traditions, eggs are even used to cleanse a person or space by absorbing negative energy.

Spellcraft Ideas: Use eggs in any meal where you want to encourage growth or mark a new chapter in life, such as a celebratory breakfast for a fresh start or new project. Cracking an egg with intention before cooking can also symbolize breaking free from old patterns.

Salt—Purification, Protection, and Preservation

Magical Properties: Salt is one of the most widely used elements in magic, symbolizing purification, grounding, and protection. Salt is believed to absorb and neutralize negative energy, which is why it is often used in cleansing rituals.

Spellcraft Ideas: Sprinkle salt around your kitchen as a protective barrier or add a pinch of salt to any dish to purify and ward off negativity. A simple ritual could include dissolving salt in water while visualizing it clearing away negativity.

Honey—Love, Sweetness, and Attraction

Magical Properties: Honey symbolizes love, attraction, and the sweetness of life. It's used to sweeten relationships, attract positivity, and encourage harmony. Honey also represents dedication, as bees work tirelessly to produce it.

Spellcraft Ideas: Add honey to tea or desserts to sweeten relationships or attract positive energy. Use it in spells for love or to bring peace to a household. Stir honey into drinks clockwise to amplify attraction and warmth.

Bread (and Grains)—Abundance, Community, and Sustenance

Magical Properties: Bread represents sustenance, community, and abundance, as grains have been a staple food for centuries. Bread-making rituals often honour the earth's bounty and the labour that goes into food production.

Spellcraft Ideas: Baking bread with intention can symbolize abundance and prosperity, as bread is traditionally associated with "breaking bread" and sharing with others. Add herbs to the dough for specific intentions, such as rosemary for memory or basil for wealth.

Milk (and Dairy)—Nurturing, Protection, and Purity

Magical Properties: Milk symbolizes nurturing, purity, and maternal protection. Dairy products generally carry comforting and grounding energies and are often associated with childhood and familial bonds.

Spellcraft Ideas: Use milk in comforting dishes, such as soups or baked goods, to foster a sense of nurturing or protection. A warm glass of milk with cinnamon can serve as a protective drink before bed, encouraging a peaceful night's sleep.

Rice—Prosperity, Protection, and Stability

Magical Properties: Rice is a symbol of wealth, abundance, and protection. In many cultures, rice is a staple and represents sustenance and good fortune. It's often used in rituals for attracting financial stability and prosperity.

Spellcraft Ideas: Cook rice with the intention of bringing stability and abundance. Scatter uncooked rice around the kitchen to symbolically "plant" prosperity or cook it as a grounding meal, infusing it with wishes for stability.

Chocolate—Love, Happiness, and Passion

Magical Properties: Chocolate is associated with love, happiness, and indulgence. Historically, chocolate has been linked to passion and romance and is believed to open the heart.

Spellcraft Ideas: Use chocolate in desserts with intentions for love, joy, or self-care. A piece of dark chocolate can serve as a ritual for grounding and calming. You could also make hot chocolate to invite warmth and happiness.

Vinegar—Cleansing, Transformation, and Banishing

Magical Properties: Vinegar is known for its strong cleansing and transformative properties, often used to banish negativity and cut ties with unwanted energies.

Spellcraft Ideas: Vinegar can be used in kitchen cleaning rituals or added to marinades to release negative energy or move forward from past obstacles. A splash in a salad dressing can add an element of transformation and clarity.

Olive Oil—Healing, Peace, and Unity

Magical Properties: Olive oil has long been sacred and is used for peace, healing, and unity. It's often used as anointing oil in ritual practices and is associated with Mediterranean traditions.

Spellcraft Ideas: Use olive oil in cooking as a gesture of peace and healing, such as in a shared family meal. Drizzle it over food as an offering to create unity and well-being among those who eat together. It can also be infused with herbs to make anointing oil.

Nuts—Wisdom, Fertility, and Luck

Magical Properties: Nuts, particularly almonds and walnuts, symbolize wisdom, fertility, and protection. Their hard shells are seen as protective, while the nutrient-rich kernel inside represents knowledge and abundance.

Spellcraft Ideas: Add nuts to baking or cooking to attract wisdom or good luck. Sprinkle nuts over dishes or blend them into sauces for added richness in spells for fertility and growth.

Chapter 5

THE MAGIC OF HERBS AND SPICES

Herbs and spices are foundational elements in Kitchen Witchery, and they offer a wealth of magical properties that can elevate both your cooking and your spiritual practice. Each herb has a unique energy that can support specific intentions, from promoting love and prosperity to enhancing clarity and calm. By infusing your meals with these intentions, herbs help you connect more deeply with nature's magic, grounding your work and amplifying the power of your culinary creations. In this chapter, we'll explore the magical properties of common kitchen herbs, how to use them in healing teas and infusions, and how to start an herb garden that nurtures both your spirit and your practice.

The Magical Properties of Common Kitchen Herbs

Every herb carries its distinct magical properties. When used intentionally, herbs can add more than just flavour to your meals; they bring in qualities like love, protection, and strength, turning your cooking into ritual and intention-setting. Here are some commonly used herbs in kitchen witchcraft and their magical properties:

Basil—Love, Wealth, and Protection

Properties: Basil is a versatile herb that symbolizes love, wealth, and protection. Its vibrant green leaves make it a popular choice in rituals for prosperity and harmony.

Spellcraft Ideas: Add fresh basil leaves to a pasta sauce when cooking for loved ones to enhance feelings of love and unity. You could also place a basil leaf in your wallet to attract financial prosperity or grow basil by your front door as a protective charm.

Rosemary—Clarity, Memory, and Protection

Properties: Known for its association with clarity and mental focus, rosemary is also a powerful protective herb that can be used in cleansing rituals.

Spellcraft Ideas: Create a rosemary-infused oil to drizzle over salads or roasted vegetables. As you prepare the oil, set an intention for mental clarity and focus. Rosemary tea can also be sipped before a study session or task that requires concentration.

Cinnamon—Warmth, Success, and Strength

Magical Properties: Cinnamon is a powerful spice that symbolizes warmth, prosperity, and success. Its strong, energizing energy is often used in spells to speed up results and bring fortune.

Spellcraft Ideas: Add cinnamon to baked goods or beverages to promote prosperity or sprinkle it into your morning coffee to invite success and motivation. A sprinkle of cinnamon on oatmeal or toast is perfect for a morning ritual to invite confidence and strength.

Mint—Freshness, Healing, and Clarity

Properties: Mint is refreshing and uplifting, known for its healing and clarifying qualities. It's often used to lift the spirits and improve focus.

Spellcraft Ideas: Brew mint tea to clear your mind or add fresh mint to a smoothie for a burst of energy and mental clarity. Planting mint in your kitchen or windowsill garden encourages a positive energy flow.

Thyme—Courage, Health, and Strength

Properties: Thyme is linked to courage, health, and strength and is often used in spells to promote physical and emotional resilience.

Spellcraft Ideas: Sprinkle thyme on roasted potatoes or add it to a soup when you need to boost your confidence and courage. Thyme tea can be helpful for immunity support, especially during colder months.

Lavender—Calm, Peace, and Love

Properties: Lavender is known for its calming effects, and it is ideal for promoting relaxation, peace, and love. However, be cautious when consuming or applying lavender topically, as there are indications that it may cause hormone dysregulation.

Spellcraft Ideas: Brew lavender tea for a calming ritual at the end of a stressful day, or bake lavender into cookies to share with friends as a gesture of harmony and love. You can also dry lavender and hang it in your kitchen to invite peace into the space.

Parsley—Purification, Protection, and Luck

Properties: Parsley is often associated with purification, protection, and good fortune. Its vibrant green colour makes it a symbol of growth and renewal.

Spellcraft Ideas: Add parsley to soups or salads with an intention of fresh starts and purification. When cooking for friends or family, use parsley to encourage protection and health for those who partake in the meal.

Sage—Wisdom, Purification, and Protection

Properties: Sage is strongly associated with purification and wisdom, making it ideal for removing negative energy and enhancing insight.

Spellcraft Ideas: Sage purifies foods, such as stuffing or roasting meats. Sage-infused vinegar can also be used to clean kitchen surfaces, symbolically clearing away stagnant energy. Dry a sprig of sage and keep it in your kitchen for ongoing protection.

Healing Teas and Infusions

Herbal teas and infusions are wonderful ways to incorporate the magical properties of herbs into your kitchen witch practice. These brews offer a gentle way to work with herbal energy, bringing you closer to the plants while nurturing your body and spirit. Here are a few examples:

Rosemary and Peppermint Tea—Clarity and Focus

Ingredients: 1 teaspoon fresh rosemary, 1 teaspoon fresh peppermint.

Preparation: Steep the herbs in hot water for 5 minutes. As you drink, visualize mental clarity and focus coming into your mind.

Magical Intention: This tea is ideal for mental clarity and focus. Rosemary sharpens the mind, and peppermint lifts the spirits, making this blend useful for study sessions or tasks requiring concentration.

Thyme and Lemon Balm Tea—Strength and Upliftment

Ingredients: 1 teaspoon dried thyme, 1 teaspoon fresh lemon balm.

Preparation: Steep the herbs in hot water for 5 minutes. Drink slowly, focusing on feelings of courage and resilience.

Magical Intention: This tea encourages resilience and inner strength. Thyme brings courage, while lemon balm uplifts, helping to boost both mood and immunity.

Incorporating Herbal Magic Through Infusions

Infused oils and vinegars are versatile additions to your kitchen that capture the essence of herbs. Creating herb-infused products allows you to imbue your meals with specific intentions and make each dish a part of your magical practice.

Creating Herb-Infused Oil

Ingredients: Fresh or dried rosemary, basil, thyme, or other herbs; olive oil or other cooking oil.

Preparation: Place herbs in a clean jar and cover with oil. Let the mixture sit in a cool, dark place for 1-2 weeks, shaking gently every day. Strain and store in a bottle.

Magical Intention: Use herb-infused oils for cooking to enhance flavour and infuse your meals with the magical properties of the chosen herb. For example, use rosemary oil for clarity or basil oil for love.

Creating Herb-Infused Vinegar

Ingredients: Fresh sage, thyme, or other herbs; vinegar of choice (apple cider or white wine vinegar).

Preparation: Place herbs in a jar and cover with vinegar. Seal tightly and let sit in a cool place for 1-2 weeks—strain and store in a bottle.

Magical Intention: Herb-infused vinegar is perfect for both culinary and cleaning purposes. Use sage vinegar to clean your space with purifying energy or thyme vinegar in salad dressings for strength and resilience.

Incorporating Herb Gardens in Your Kitchen

A small herb garden is one of the most powerful ways to deepen your connection to nature and integrate herbal magic into your kitchen. By growing your own herbs, you have fresh cooking ingredients and cultivate a relationship with the plants, enhancing their magical effects. Here's how to get started:

Choosing Herbs for Your Garden

Start with a few easy-to-grow herbs that resonate with your intentions. Some excellent beginner-friendly options include:

- Basil for love and wealth.

- Rosemary for clarity and protection.

- Mint for healing and clarity.

- Thyme for courage and strength.

- Sage for wisdom and purification.

Creating a Ritual Around Growing and Harvesting

Treat your herb garden as a magical practice. As you place each plant in the soil, set an intention for it, giving thanks for its energy and asking it to support your magical goals.

Harvesting can also be a sacred act. When you clip fresh basil leaves or rosemary sprigs, do so mindfully and with gratitude, acknowledging the energy they bring to your food and spells.

Indoor and Outdoor Options

A windowsill is perfect for an indoor herb garden, allowing you to grow plants year-round. If you have outdoor space, consider expanding your herb garden to include other magical plants, like lavender or chamomile, which thrive in the sun and enhance your connection to the seasons.

Embracing the Natural World in Your Kitchen Practice

Incorporating herbs and spices into your kitchen witchcraft enhances your meals and connects you to the earth's rhythms. Every time you cook with fresh herbs or sip an herbal tea, you engage in a ritual honouring the natural world. By intentionally using these ingredients, you're embracing nature's gifts and grounding yourself in mindful, magical cooking.

Whether you're growing a small herb garden, preparing healing teas, or infusing oils, each practice deepens your relationship with the plants and their energies. Herbs' magic is accessible to anyone willing to work with them, and by bringing them into your kitchen, you transform everyday cooking into an act of connection, healing, and magic.

Herbs are central to kitchen witchery because of their culinary uses and magical properties. Incorporating herbs into your cooking can amplify the energy of your meals.

Chapter 6

KITCHEN MAGIC FOR MENTAL HEALTH AND SELF-CARE—THE MAGIC OF SHAPES

I n Kitchen Witchery, every detail in food preparation can hold magical significance, transforming everyday cooking into an act of intention and self-care.
Food shapes, whether pasta, vegetables, or baked goods, carry symbolic meanings
rooted in cultural beliefs, spiritual traditions, and the natural world. By being
mindful of the shapes in your cooking, you can amplify specific intentions, turning each meal into a unique ritual that supports mental well-being and self-care.

This chapter explores how various shapes of foods can symbolize different
energies, helping you align your meals with your mental and emotional goals.
From spaghetti's unifying energy to cubes' grounding stability, each shape offers
an opportunity to personalize your cooking with magic that nurtures both body
and spirit.

The Magic of Pasta Shapes

Pasta shapes are a versatile element in the kitchen, each with unique symbolism
that can help support your emotional and mental well-being. Here are some
popular shapes and how they can be used in magical self-care:

Spaghetti—Connection and Harmony

Meaning: Long and slender, spaghetti is associated with unity, relationships, and connection.

Spellcraft Ideas: Spaghetti is ideal for meals shared with loved ones, promoting harmony and connection. When you cook spaghetti, take a moment to set an intention for unity, whether within a relationship, family, or even between your mind and heart.

Penne—Motivation and Progress

Meaning: The diagonal cut of penne suggests movement and forward momentum.

Spellcraft Ideas: Use penne when you need a motivational boost. It's an excellent choice when you're seeking to push through obstacles or embark on a new venture. Imagine each piece of penne as a step forward, helping you stay determined and energized.

Fusilli (Spiral Pasta)—Transformation and Growth

Meaning: The spiral shape of fusilli represents cycles and the flow of life.

Spellcraft Ideas: Fusilli is perfect for spells or meals focused on change, growth, and evolution. If you're going through a period of personal transformation, cook with fusilli to symbolize moving with life's twists and turns. Visualize each spiral as a stage in your journey, leading you toward positive growth.

Stars (Star-Shaped Pasta)—Hope and Aspiration

Meaning: Stars symbolize dreams, guidance, and hope.

Spellcraft Ideas: Star-shaped pasta is perfect when you're setting intentions for goals and dreams. Make a star-themed pasta dish when focusing on a new aspiration, and let each star remind you of your dreams and the hope needed to bring them to life.

The Symbolism of Vegetable Cuts

Vegetable cuts add an extra layer of intention to meals. By choosing specific shapes, you can infuse your cooking with energy that supports your mental and emotional health. Bonus: Different cuts provide depth in texture, resulting in a more enjoyable meal.

Cubes—Stability and Grounding

Meaning: Cubes are sturdy and balanced, representing stability and grounding.

Spellcraft Ideas: Cube-cut vegetables like potatoes, squash, or carrots bring grounding energy to meals. Use cubes when you need stability, such as before a challenging day or when you feel emotionally scattered. Focus on each cube as a symbol of a steady foundation, helping you feel anchored and secure.

Sticks (Julienne)—Clarity and Focus

Meaning: Long, thin shapes like sticks suggest sharpness, clarity, and focus.

Spellcraft Ideas: Use stick-cut vegetables like carrots or bell peppers to enhance mental clarity and concentration. This shape is excellent for meals prepared before studying or work, as it supports sharpness of mind. Visualize the thin, clear lines helping you cut through distractions.

Rounds (Sliced)—Wholeness and Cycles

Meaning: Round shapes represent wholeness, completion, and cycles.

Spellcraft Ideas: Slices of tomatoes, cucumbers, or zucchini remind us of life's cyclical nature. Use rounds to support rituals of closure or personal completion, helping you feel whole and balanced. Imagine each round as a reminder of life's rhythms and the fulfilment of your goals.

Whole—Integrity and Protection

Meaning: Whole vegetables symbolize completeness, integrity, and protection.

Spellcraft Ideas: Whole vegetables like pumpkins, apples, or squash carry protective energy. Use them in rituals or meals when you need to feel safeguarded and whole. Imagine the entire vegetable as a shield, representing the power of self-care and self-protection. Consider serving a pumpkin soup in a pumpkin, or stuffed peppers or tomatoes.

Mashed—Comfort and Nurturing

Meaning: Mashed foods are soft, symbolizing comfort, nurturing, and emotional care.

Spellcraft Ideas: Mashed foods like potatoes or sweet potatoes are ideal for self-care meals focused on emotional nourishment. Use them when you need extra comfort or are working on self-soothing. Imagine each spoonful as an embrace, offering warmth and grounding during times of stress.

General Shapes and Their Meanings

Outside of pasta and vegetable cuts, various shapes hold symbolic meanings that can enhance the magical properties of your food. Here are some common shapes and how they can support your mental health and self-care:

Triangles: Often associated with transformation and new beginnings, triangular shapes can represent the three phases of life—birth, growth, and transformation. Foods, like pizza slices, can be used in rituals for new starts or self-discovery, symbolizing each stage of your journey.

Hearts: Heart shapes are universal symbols of love, affection, and emotional connection. Foods cut or shaped like hearts (like heart-shaped cookies) are perfect for love spells, self-compassion, or bonding with others. Use heart-shaped foods when setting intentions for relationships with yourself and others.

Waves: Foods with wavelike patterns (like bread or certain pastries) suggest flow and adaptability, supporting flexibility and resilience. If you're working on adaptability or going through life changes, foods with this shape can remind you to flow gracefully through life's currents.

Practical Applications of Shape Magic in Cooking

The beauty of shape magic is that it transforms even the simplest meal into a personalized ritual for mental and emotional well-being. Below are some practical ways to integrate shape magic into your cooking:

Setting Intentions

Before you start cooking, consider the intention you want to bring into the meal. Are you seeking clarity, comfort, or motivation? Let your intention guide your choice of shapes. For example, if you're aiming for clarity, julienne (stick-cut) vegetables to focus on their sharpness and precision.

Ritualistic Cutting

As you chop and prepare ingredients, visualize each shape amplifying your intention. For grounding, cube your vegetables with mindful, steady cuts. For cycles or wholeness, slice your vegetables into rounds, seeing each slice as a reminder of life's natural rhythm. Cutting vegetables this way turns preparation into a meditative ritual.

Plating with Purpose

How you present food on the plate can enhance the meal's meaning. Arrange foods intentionally, such as placing circular slices together to symbolize unity or pairing heart-shaped items for love and connection. By mindfully plating with shape symbolism, you visually represent your goals.

Creating Shape-Centred Meals

Consider making an entire meal focused on a single shape for special intentions. For example, a dinner of spiral pasta, spiral-cut vegetables, and a dessert with swirling whipped cream can symbolize transformation and change. This approach is compelling when marking significant life events or working on personal growth.

Bringing Magic and Self-Care into Every Meal

The magic of shapes in Kitchen Witchery is a subtle yet powerful way to incorporate intention into cooking. By aligning food shapes with your mental health and self-care goals, you can enhance the energy of your meals, turning everyday cooking into a mindful and magical practice. Remember that Kitchen Witchery isn't about perfection but connecting with the magic already around you.

So the next time you cook, consider the shapes you're using and how they can support your emotional and mental well-being. Whether you're slicing vegetables, boiling pasta, or baking, these shapes add layers of meaning, making each meal a small ritual of care, intention, and healing. Through the magic of shapes, your kitchen becomes a sanctuary where you can nurture both body and spirit.

Chapter 7

THE POWER OF COLOUR MAGIC IN KITCHEN WITCHERY

C olour is a potent tool in magic, and in the kitchen, it can bring energy, focus, and intention to everything you create. Each colour has its symbolism and vibration, influencing mood and energy. By choosing ingredients, setting the table, or even serving dishes with certain colours, a Kitchen Witch can amplify the intentions behind a meal. Whether cooking for love, protection, healing, or abundance, colour magic adds a vibrant layer to your kitchen witchcraft, helping you bring more depth and power to every meal.

This chapter will explore how to use colour magic in your kitchen, from ingredient choices to table arrangements. You don't need to overhaul your space or buy new tools—just a few mindful choices can help you channel colour energy to match your intentions.

Understanding Colour Meanings in Kitchen Witchery

Below are common colours and their magical meanings, along with examples of how to incorporate them into your kitchen practice.

Red: Passion, vitality, courage
Orange: Creativity, joy, enthusiasm
Yellow: Happiness, mental clarity, confidence
Green: Healing, growth, abundance
Blue: Calm, communication, peace

Purple: Spirituality, intuition, wisdom
White: Purity, protection, clarity
Black: Grounding, strength, protection

Using Colour Magic Through Ingredients

One of the easiest and most accessible ways to harness colour magic in the kitchen is through ingredients. Fruits, vegetables, and herbs naturally come in various colours, each carrying energy that aligns with various magical intentions. By selecting ingredients based on colour, you can infuse your meal with specific vibrations and amplify the meal's purpose.

Red—Passion and Vitality

Ingredients: tomatoes, strawberries, red bell peppers, raspberries, cherries.

Spellcraft Ideas: Red ingredients are great for spells of love, courage, and strength. Use tomatoes and red peppers in a vibrant pasta sauce for a romantic meal, or prepare a strawberry dessert intending to enhance love and passion. If you're cooking for confidence, adding a few red ingredients can help bring that courageous energy into the dish.

Orange—Creativity and Joy

Ingredients: carrots, oranges, sweet potatoes, mangoes, apricots.

Spellcraft Ideas: Orange ingredients are wonderful for creativity and joy. Prepare a carrot soup or sweet potato mash when you need an energy boost or want to spark creativity. A fruit salad with oranges and mangoes can be perfect for a gathering where you want to foster fun and laughter.

Yellow—Happiness and Clarity

Ingredients: lemons, corn, bananas, yellow bell peppers, pineapple.

Spellcraft Ideas: Yellow ingredients are ideal for happiness, mental clarity, and boosting self-confidence. Squeeze lemon into water for a cleansing ritual, or serve a pineapple dessert to lift the mood. Yellow foods bring an uplifting energy perfect for brightening spirits or celebrating positive moments.

Green—Healing and Abundance

Ingredients: spinach, kale, avocados, zucchini, peas, herbs like basil and parsley.

Spellcraft Ideas: Green ingredients are essential for health, healing, and prosperity. Choose green ingredients when cooking a meal intended to foster growth or healing, like a nourishing soup. A fresh salad with avocado and greens is perfect for abundance, or add herbs like basil to pasta for luck and prosperity.

Blue—Calm and Communication

Ingredients: blueberries, blue corn, elderberries.

Spellcraft Ideas: Blue foods are rare but powerful for calming and promoting peaceful communication. Incorporate blueberries into desserts or make tea with elderberries to encourage honest and open communication. Blue foods are ideal for gatherings where peaceful, heart-centred conversation is needed.

Purple—Spirituality and Intuition

Ingredients: purple cabbage, eggplant, grapes, plums.

Spellcraft Ideas: Purple ingredients enhance spirituality, intuition, and wisdom. Add purple foods like eggplant or grapes when making a meal meant for introspection or meditation. Lavender can be added to baked goods for a peaceful, spiritual connection, or purple cabbage can be used in a salad to promote insight and mental clarity.

White—Purity and Protection

Ingredients: cauliflower, garlic, onions, mushrooms, milk and milk substitutes.

Spellcraft Ideas: White foods symbolize protection, clarity, and new beginnings. Use garlic and onions to add protection and ward off negativity, or make a cauliflower dish for a meal focusing on purity and renewal. White foods are perfect for meals prepared with the intention of starting fresh or creating a protective barrier.

Black—Grounding and Strength

Ingredients: black beans, blackberries, black rice, dark chocolate.

Spellcraft Ideas: Black ingredients are grounding and protective, great for meals intended to provide strength or endurance. Black beans in a stew can help you stay grounded, while blackberries in a dessert can symbolize inner strength. Use black ingredients for spells related to protection and grounding.

Colour Magic in Table Settings and Serving Dishes

Besides ingredient choices, colour magic can extend to table settings and serving dishes. Plates, cups, napkins, and even tablecloths can add another layer of intention to your meals. Using colour in your table décor allows you to channel your intentions through the environment you create, making the meal an immersive magical experience. Below are suggestions that can be mixed or matched. Consider a table setting in one colour or multicolour and the impact of your spell.

Red Tableware—Energy and Passion

For a romantic dinner, use red plates or a tablecloth to amplify passion and love. Red candles on the table can intensify the energy and create an atmosphere of warmth and affection.

Orange Accents—Creativity and Connection

Orange napkins, placemats, or candles can add an energetic and creative vibe to a gathering, encouraging conversation and joy. Use orange accents for celebrations, birthdays, or any time you want to inspire fun and connection.

Yellow Decor—Happiness and Positivity

A yellow table runner or yellow serving dishes can uplift the mood and brighten the space. Yellow is ideal for gatherings aimed at spreading positivity or celebrating successes. It's also a great choice for brunches, where the intention is to begin the day with joy.

Green Elements—Healing and Prosperity

Green bowls, plants, or even fresh herbs on the table add a sense of growth, health, and prosperity to the space. For a meal focused on abundance or healing, place small sprigs of fresh herbs or leaves on each plate, or use green plates and cups.

Blue Accents—Calm and Communication

Blue plates, glasses, or even a blue centrepiece can create a calming atmosphere, encouraging open and relaxed communication. Blue is perfect for meals where you want to foster understanding, such as a family discussion or an intimate gathering.

Purple Centrepiece—Spiritual Connection

Purple napkins, candles, or tablecloths create a magical, spiritual ambiance. A purple setting can elevate the energy for meals focused on intuition or inner peace, making it ideal for dinners meant to inspire reflection.

White Tablescape—for New Beginnings and Simplicity

White plates, tablecloths, and candles create an atmosphere of simplicity, purity, and elegance. Use white settings when celebrating new beginnings or marking important life changes, such as a wedding or housewarming.

Black Crockery—for Grounding and Protection

Black dishes, candles, or a dark tablecloth bring grounding energy to your meals. Use black accents for gatherings focused on stability, protection, or endings, such as a farewell meal or a meal before a challenging event.

Creating a Multicolour Meal for Holistic Intentions

Sometimes, your intention for a meal may span multiple areas, such as hosting a family dinner that brings warmth, joy, and calm all at once. In such cases, creating a multi-colour meal can encompass different intentions, helping you channel diverse energies into one harmonious meal. For example, a salad with greens (for health), red tomatoes (for love), and yellow bell peppers (for positivity) can bring in varied energies while remaining cohesive.

Consider blending colours on the table as well, using plates, napkins, or candles in complementary shades that align with the multiple intentions you're bringing into the meal. A multi-colour approach allows you to create a well-rounded magical experience that touches on all aspects of well-being and connection.

Colour magic is an accessible and powerful way to infuse your kitchen witchery with intention. By choosing ingredients, dishes, and table settings that align with your goals, you can amplify the energy and purpose behind your meals. From the food on your plate to the colours that decorate your table, colour magic offers a simple, customizable way to bring magic into every meal. So next time you cook, let colour guide your choices and embrace the beauty and power it brings to your sacred kitchen space.

Chapter 8

KITCHEN WITCHERY AND THE MAGIC OF REDUCING FOOD WASTE

In kitchen witchery, food isn't just fuel; it's a gift from nature, a resource that requires respect and appreciation. Reducing food waste is a way to practice mindfulness, honour every ingredient, and make the most of what the earth has provided. For a kitchen witch, this approach is more than just being environmentally friendly—it's a way of working in harmony with nature, valuing each vegetable, herb, and grain that enters the kitchen. Reducing waste can turn cooking into an intentional ritual that celebrates abundance, resourcefulness, and conservation.

This chapter explores the role of food waste reduction in kitchen witchery, offering practical ways to incorporate mindful use of ingredients and creative ideas for extending the life of foods in ways that align with your magic. From root-to-stem cooking to revitalizing leftovers, you'll find that reducing waste can be a powerful part of your kitchen practice.

Why Should a Kitchen Witch Care About Food Waste?

Food waste is a widespread issue in modern society, where it's all too common for perfectly edible food to be discarded. This disregard for ingredients overlooks the energy, time, and resources required to produce them. Each plant, fruit, grain, or herb is a product of nature's cycles, from sun and soil to water and growth, which deserve our respect and appreciation. For a kitchen witch, wasting food means disconnecting from these natural cycles and disregarding the value that these ingredients hold.

Honouring the earth's resources is essential to kitchen witchery, as the practice itself is rooted in respect for nature. By consciously reducing food waste, you're not only lessening your environmental impact but also deepening your connection to nature and the magical energy of the ingredients. This act of conservation is a way to align with the natural cycles of growth, harvest, and renewal, recognizing that each ingredient holds potential and purpose.

Reducing waste is also a form of gratitude. When we use every part of an ingredient, we express appreciation for what nature has provided. It's an act of reciprocity, giving back to the earth by valuing its resources fully and creatively.

Practical Ways to Incorporate Food Waste Reduction into Kitchen Witchery

There are many ways to incorporate waste reduction into your kitchen witch practice. By focusing on using every part of an ingredient, planning meals with mindfulness, and getting creative with leftovers, you can turn food conservation into a ritual of intention and respect.

Root-to-Stem Cooking

Root-to-stem cooking is a practice that uses every edible part of a plant. This approach minimizes waste and also adds variety and flavour to your dishes. Many parts of plants that are commonly discarded—like carrot tops, beet greens, and broccoli stems—are not only edible but delicious and nutritious.

Ideas for Root-to-Stem Cooking

Carrot Tops: Use carrot tops to make a bright, herbaceous pesto. Blend them with olive oil, garlic, nuts, and a sprinkle of salt for a spread or pasta sauce full of earthy flavour and grounding energy.

Beet Greens: Beet greens are flavourful and packed with nutrients. Sauté them with garlic and olive oil, adding a pinch of salt for purification. They can be used as a side dish or a base for a grain bowl, symbolizing health and vitality.

Broccoli Stems: Peel the tough outer layer and slice the stems thinly. They can be added to stir-fries, roasted, or blended into soups, bringing balance and adaptability into your meals.

By honouring the whole plant, you deepen your relationship with nature and use ingredients to their fullest potential, making each meal a ritual of appreciation and resourcefulness.

Preserving Ingredients for Later Use

Preserving food helps to extend the life of ingredients and keep them from going to waste. Simple preservation methods like freezing, drying, or fermenting align with kitchen witchery by honouring seasonal abundance and storing the energy of an ingredient for future use.

Preservation Techniques

Freezing: Herbs that are close to wilting can be chopped and frozen in olive oil in ice cube trays. These herb cubes are perfect for adding a burst of flavour to soups and sauces. Each frozen cube preserves summer's vitality for colder months.

Drying: Herbs like rosemary, thyme, or oregano can be tied and hung to dry. Once dried, they can be stored for use in cooking or rituals throughout the year, bringing the essence of their season into your practice.

Fermenting: Fermentation not only preserves food but transforms it, much like a magical process of change and renewal. Fermented foods like sauerkraut or kimchi add depth to your meals, symbolizing resilience and adaptability.

These preservation methods allow you to honour abundance by keeping seasonal ingredients available year-round. Each preserved ingredient carries a reminder of the earth's cycles and the energy of the season it was harvested in.

Reimagining Leftovers

Leftovers are often overlooked, but treating them with intention and creativity can transform them into new dishes that feel fresh and purposeful. Leftovers hold the energy of the previous meal, and revitalizing them creates continuity in your kitchen practice.

Creative Ways to Use Leftovers

Transform Vegetables into Soup: Leftover roasted vegetables can be blended into a comforting soup with broth, garlic, and herbs. This dish not only warms the body but repurposes food with gratitude.

Revive Rice as a Stir-Fry: Rice from a previous meal can be turned into a colourful stir-fry with fresh vegetables, soy sauce, and a dash of sesame oil. This is a symbol of adaptability, creating something entirely new from an existing base.

Bread into Croutons: Stale bread can be cubed and baked into croutons, perfect for salads and soups. Bread represents abundance and grounding, and by repurposing it, you're extending the life of a staple ingredient.

By seeing leftovers as an opportunity to create something new, you honour the abundance you already have and keep waste to a minimum. This practice is both economical and magical, connecting meals through intention and continuity.

Embracing Food Waste Reduction as a Mindful Practice

Reducing food waste isn't about striving for perfection; it's about fostering a mindful approach to ingredients. By valuing each part of the ingredient and looking for ways to use it to its fullest, you become more aware of the interconnectedness of nature, food, and your own practice.

Setting Intentions for Conservation

When you cook, take a moment to set an intention for conservation. This could be a simple affirmation, such as, "I honour the abundance of the earth," or a more specific focus, like using up vegetables before they go bad. Setting this intention brings purpose to your actions and keeps conservation at the forefront of your practice.

Expressing Gratitude

Expressing gratitude for each ingredient is a beautiful way to acknowledge its journey and the resources it took to reach your kitchen. Before a meal, you might thank the earth, the growers, and even the plant or animal itself, recognizing the interconnected efforts that made the meal possible. This gratitude amplifies the energy in your kitchen and creates a deeper connection with each dish.

Recipes for Food Waste Reduction

Here are a few recipes designed to minimize waste, honour seasonal abundance, and infuse your cooking with conservation-minded magic.

Vegetable Scrap Broth—Grounding, Resourcefulness, and Conservation

Ingredients:
- Vegetable scraps (carrot tops, onion skins, celery ends, herb stems)

- Water

- 2 garlic cloves (protection)

- 1 bay leaf (wisdom)

- Salt and pepper to taste

Instructions:
1. Collect vegetable scraps over the week, storing them in the freezer until you have enough for a broth.

2. Add the scraps, garlic, and bay leaf to a pot of water, setting an intention for conservation and grounding.

3. Simmer for 1–2 hours, then strain and season. Use this broth as a base for soups, infusing your meals with the essence of resourcefulness.

Herb Oil Cubes—Preservation, Healing, and Adaptability

Ingredients:

- Fresh herbs (basil, parsley, rosemary)

- Olive oil

Instructions:

1. Chop herbs and place them in ice cube trays. Cover with olive oil, setting an intention for preservation and healing.

2. Freeze and use as needed to add flavour and energy to dishes, keeping the essence of the herbs alive long after their season.

When Food Goes Bad: Returning to the Earth

Even with the best intentions, there will be times when food goes past its prime. In kitchen witchcraft, handling food waste mindfully is essential, as well as acknowledging the energy and resources that go into producing each ingredient. Rather than simply discarding spoiled food in the trash, where it will likely end up in a landfill, consider ways to return it to the earth, creating a cycle that nurtures nature rather than harming it. Below are several practical and magical ways to honour food even when it's no longer edible.

Composting: Transforming Waste into Nutrients

Composting is a powerful way to recycle organic matter, returning nutrients to the soil and supporting future growth. By composting food scraps and spoiled ingredients, you're giving them a new purpose and continuing the natural cycle of growth, decay, and rebirth.

How to Start Composting

Kitchen Compost Bin: Begin with a small compost bin or container on your kitchen counter to collect scraps like vegetable peels, coffee grounds, and eggshells. Avoid adding meat, dairy, or oily foods to keep the compost healthy and odour-free.

Outdoor Compost Pile or Bin: If you have outdoor space, consider setting up a compost pile or bin where these scraps can decompose. Over time, the organic matter will break down into nutrient-rich soil.

Community Compost Programs: If you don't have outdoor space, many communities have compost drop-off locations or services that collect kitchen scraps for local gardens or farms.

As you add scraps to your compost, set an intention for renewal and gratitude. Visualize the nutrients returning to the earth, supporting new growth and completing the cycle of life.

Creating Natural Cleaners from Food Scraps

Some food scraps can be repurposed into effective, eco-friendly cleaners. Citrus peels, for instance, have natural antibacterial properties and can be transformed into a multi-purpose cleaner with just a few simple steps. This approach helps reduce waste while creating a cleaner free of harsh chemicals, which is ideal for a kitchen, which is a sacred space.

DIY Citrus Cleaner Recipe

Collect citrus peels (lemon, orange, or grapefruit) and place them in a jar.

Cover the peels with white vinegar, sealing the jar and letting it sit for two weeks.

Strain the liquid, dilute it with equal parts water, and use it as an all-purpose cleaner for countertops and surfaces.

By turning food scraps into a cleaner, you're respecting the usefulness of every ingredient and creating a natural tool for purification and protection within your kitchen.

Feeding the Garden: Natural Fertilizers and Pest Deterrents

Certain food scraps are fantastic for garden health, and using them this way can make your garden an extension of your kitchen magic. Eggs, coffee grounds, and even banana peels offer nutrients that plants love, helping you to enrich your garden in simple, sustainable ways.

Ideas for Garden-Friendly Food Waste

Eggshells: Crushed eggshells add calcium to the soil and help prevent rot in plants like tomatoes. Scatter them around plants as a natural nutrient boost.

Coffee Grounds: Used coffee grounds can be added to soil to increase acidity, making them perfect for acid-loving plants like roses and hydrangeas.

Banana Peels: Soak banana peels in water and then use the infused water to water your plants. This adds potassium and other nutrients to the soil, supporting healthy growth.

As you use food waste to nourish your garden, focus on the intention of supporting life and creating a natural cycle of abundance.

Magically Returning Food to Nature

Even when food is no longer suitable for eating, it can still play a role in your kitchen witch practice. Fruits, herbs, and other ingredients can be returned to nature in small rituals that honour the earth. For example, burying certain fruits or herbs in a garden or planting a tree with leftover seeds can symbolize gratitude, growth, and renewal.

Simple Return-to-Earth Ritual

Choose an area of your garden, yard, or even a potted plant.

Take spoiled herbs, fruit peels, or vegetable scraps and bury them in the soil.

As you cover the scraps, set an intention for renewal, gratitude, and growth, acknowledging the earth's cycle.

This practice turns food waste into an offering, a way of giving back to the earth as a thank-you for all it has provided.

Embracing a Full-Cycle Approach to Kitchen Witchery

In kitchen witchery, every part of food's journey—from preparation and enjoyment to decomposition—has value. When we find ways to honour even spoiled food, we close the loop, creating a respectful cycle that honours the earth, minimizes waste, and supports sustainable practices. By composting, creating natural cleaners, feeding our gardens, and returning ingredients to nature, we align ourselves with the cycles of growth, decay, and rebirth.

Remember, kitchen magic is about more than just the meals you create—it's about the relationships you build with the natural world and the energy you bring to every part of the process. By reducing waste and honouring every ingredient, you deepen your connection to the earth and reinforce the values of conservation, respect, and gratitude in your kitchen witch practice.

The Magic of Conservation in Kitchen Witchery

Reducing food waste is a natural extension of kitchen witchery, a practice rooted in valuing what nature provides and using it mindfully. Each ingredient is a resource to be respected and appreciated, from the root to the stem. Through mindful use of ingredients, preservation, and creative repurposing, kitchen witches can bring conservation into their everyday practice, aligning with nature's cycles and honouring abundance.

By embracing waste reduction, you not only lessen your impact on the environment but create meals that are more intentional, magical, and respectful of the natural world. Let every meal, from start to finish, become a celebration of nature's gifts, a practice of gratitude, and a symbol of respect for the resources that sustain us.

Part 2

RITUALS FOR MENTAL HEALTH AND WELL-BEING

Chapter 9

KITCHEN MAGIC, MENTAL HEALTH, AND THE ART OF COOKING FROM SCRATCH

C ooking from scratch can be a deeply fulfilling practice that nurtures both body and soul. In Kitchen Witchery, making homemade foods like bread, pasta, jams, and more becomes a ritual of mindfulness and self-care. These traditional processes connect us to the past, ground us in the present, and provide a sense of accomplishment and satisfaction that fosters mental well-being. This chapter explores the therapeutic benefits of creating foods from scratch, its mental health boosts, and how to infuse each recipe with intention and magic. Remember, doing everything from scratch is unnecessary; shortcuts help save time and reduce stress. Only take on the challenge of cooking from scratch when you have the time and patience to do so. Not everyone has to nurture a sourdough starter for years making fresh bread; sometimes, it is as easy as grabbing a bunch of fruit before it goes bad and making fruit leather.

The Mental Health Benefits of Cooking from Scratch

Cooking from scratch allows you to slow down, focus on each step, and savour creating something with your own hands. This mindful approach to cooking can reduce stress, elevate mood, and increase feelings of self-worth. When you knead dough, stir a pot, or carefully slice ingredients, you enter a state of flow—a mental state where time fades away and you're fully absorbed in the task at hand. These moments of mindfulness are grounding, helping to release tension and promote relaxation.

Sense of Achievement: Completing a recipe from scratch gives a sense of accomplishment, boosting self-confidence.

Mindful Presence: The steps involved in scratch cooking, like kneading or chopping, invite you to be fully present, easing worry and stress.

Connecting with Tradition: Traditional recipes link you to past generations, bringing continuity and grounding.

Bread-Making: Kneading Magic and Grounding Energy

Bread-making is one of the most magical and grounding forms of cooking. The process of mixing, kneading, and baking can be a form of meditation, helping you connect with the earth's energies and your own intentions. Each ingredient carries symbolism—flour represents abundance, yeast symbolizes growth, and salt purifies. Combined and baked, they create a product that nourishes both body and spirit.

During my second year at university, I cooked all the bread for the household from scratch. Despite having a full course load and working what felt like full-time hours to pay for my education, I still set aside time for bread making. It was my time to reflect on what I was learning, develop my perspectives on topics, and feel a sense of accomplishment when the bread came out of the oven. The entire process of feeding the yeast, mixing, kneading, and watching it grow and cook that was so rewarding.

Simple Homemade Bread—Grounding, Growth, and Abundance

Ingredients:
- 3 cups flour (abundance and grounding)

- 1 cup warm water (flexibility and adaptability)

- 1 packet of yeast (growth and transformation)

- 1 teaspoon salt (purification)

- 1 tablespoon honey (sweetness and connection)

Instructions:

1. Mix flour, yeast, and salt in a large bowl. Add warm water and honey, kneading the dough until it's smooth and elastic. As you knead, focus on grounding and growth, visualizing any tension releasing from your body.

2. Let the dough rise in a warm place, setting an intention for abundance and nurturing.

3. Bake at 350°F (175°C) until golden brown, embracing the comforting aroma of freshly baked bread. As you eat, savour the energy of nourishment and warmth.

Pasta Making—Creativity, Playfulness, and Resilience

Making pasta from scratch allows you to engage in a creative, hands-on process that boosts resilience and joy. The act of rolling, shaping, and forming pasta is both playful and therapeutic, letting you explore your creative side while focusing on the task. Fresh pasta carries a different energy than store-bought—it's infused with your intention, your energy, and the love you put into its creation.

Once you are comfortable with a simple pasta, you can infuse the dough with colour, for example, using beet juice or pureed spinach, to add depth to your spell crafting.

Homemade Pasta—Creativity, Patience, and Joy

Ingredients:

- 2 cups flour (abundance and grounding)

- 3 large eggs (new beginnings and fertility)

- A pinch of salt (purification and balance)

Instructions:

1. Create a well in the center of the flour, adding eggs and salt. Mix with your hands, embracing the feeling of the dough coming together.

2. Knead the dough until smooth, then let it rest. Use this resting time to set an intention for creativity and resilience.

3. Roll out the dough and cut it into your desired shapes, allowing yourself to enjoy the process without focusing on perfection.

4. Cook the pasta and savour each bite, appreciating the playful, handmade nature of the dish.

Fruit Leather: Preservation, Patience, and Transformation

Fruit leather is a wonderful example of food preservation, symbolizing patience, care, and transformation. It is also an example of a little effort with a big reward.

Slowly drying fruit preserves its natural sweetness and concentrates its flavour, turning simple ingredients into a delicious, nutritious treat. This process can be an exercise in mindfulness, patience, and the magic of preserving life's sweetness.

I prefer adding a small apple to my fruit leather mixture to increase the natural pectin and help with the setting. The rest of the fruits can vary each time.

Homemade Fruit Leather—Preservation, Patience, and Gratitude

Ingredients:
- 3 cups fresh or frozen fruit (joy and abundance)
- Squeeze of lemon juice (cleansing and purification) - optional
- 1 tablespoon honey or maple syrup (sweetness and harmony)

Instructions:
1. Chop larger fruits (kiwis, apples...) into small pieces. Aim to have all the pieces about the same size, maybe a little smaller for dense fruits like apples.

2. In a pot on the stovetop or microwave, cook the fruit slowly on low heat as it starts releasing juices. Stir often to avoid scorching. Add the lemon juice and sweetener if using.

3. Cook the fruit on medium-low to help evaporate some of the liquid and soften harder fruits.

4. Blend the fruit and sweetener, focusing on gratitude for nature's bounty.

5. To create a smoother fruit leather, you can pass the mixture through a sieve, removing any unblended fruit and tiny seeds (berries and kiwis)

6. Spread the mixture thinly on a baking sheet lined with parchment paper.

7. Bake at the lowest setting (around 140°F or 60°C) for 6–8 hours. My oven only starts at 170°F so I leave the door cracked. As it dries, set an intention for patience and transformation, imagining the fruit's flavour concentrating and developing.

8. Once dry, cut the fruit leather into strips, wrapping them up as small symbols of life's preserved sweetness.

Salsas and Sauces: Blending Flavours and Vibrant Energy

Making salsas and sauces from scratch is an energizing ritual, bringing together bold flavours and vibrant colours. You can create dishes full of life, energy, and intention by chopping, blending, and combining fresh ingredients. These recipes symbolize adaptability, unity, and zest, and they're perfect for infusing your food with joy and liveliness.

Fresh Salsa—Energy, Zest, and Connection

Ingredients:
- 2 ripe tomatoes, diced (love and vitality)

- 1/2 onion, diced (clarity and courage)

- 1 jalapeño pepper, minced (passion and intensity)

- 1/4 cup fresh cilantro, chopped (healing and cleansing)

- Juice of 1 lime (clarity and energy)

- Salt to taste

Instructions:
- Combine all ingredients in a bowl, visualizing energy and connection as you mix.

- Taste and adjust seasoning, allowing your intuition to guide you in achieving balance.

- Serve with intention, embracing the vibrant flavours and joy of fresh ingredients.

Homemade Jams and Preserves: Holding Onto Sweetness and Memories

Preserving fruits as jams and spreads is a beautiful ritual that symbolizes holding onto sweetness and savouring life's moments. By capturing the essence of seasonal fruits, you're preserving the memory of a particular time and season. This ritual is both practical and magical, creating something that you can return to even after the season has passed.

Strawberry Jam—Sweetness, Memory, and Abundance

Ingredients:
- 2 cups fresh strawberries, hulled (love and joy)

- 1 cup sugar (sweetness and connection)

- 1 tablespoon lemon juice (clarity and freshness)

Instructions:
1. Mash strawberries with sugar in a pot, bringing it to a gentle boil. As you stir, reflect on the sweetness of life and the memories you want to hold close.

2. Add lemon juice and simmer, stirring occasionally, until the jam thickens.

3. Pour into jars, sealing the sweetness and joy to enjoy later as a reminder of abundance.

Infusing Intention into Scratch Cooking

Cooking from scratch is an ideal opportunity to infuse intention into your food. By focusing on your energy and goals, you can create dishes that serve as more than just nourishment—they become tools for manifestation, healing, and grounding. Here are a few ideas to keep in mind as you cook:

Set an Intention for Each Recipe: Whether it's grounding, healing, or joy, set an intention before you begin. Visualize this energy being absorbed by each ingredient.

Use Mindful Movements: Kneading, stirring, chopping, and rolling all carry energy. Engage with each movement, letting it become a form of meditation.

Express Gratitude: Take a moment to express gratitude for each ingredient, appreciating the journey it took to reach your kitchen.

The Therapeutic Nature of Cooking from Scratch

Making foods like bread, pasta, and jams from scratch is a therapeutic practice that strengthens mental health, self-connection, and resilience. These hands-on recipes offer you a space to unwind, connect with the present, and find joy in the simple act of creation. Cooking from scratch reminds us that food is not just fuel but an experience—a ritual that brings us closer to ourselves, our communities, and the natural world.

Each time you cook from scratch, you engage in a practice that's deeply personal and rich with intention, helping you feel grounded, fulfilled, and connected. Embrace this journey as a part of your self-care and kitchen witchery, finding peace and purpose in each lovingly crafted dish.

Chapter 10

MINDFUL COOKING AS MEDITATION

C ooking can be a powerful form of meditation, an opportunity to focus the mind, ground the spirit, and infuse each meal with intention. In Kitchen Witchery, every action taken in the kitchen can be transformed into a ritual that nurtures both body and soul. Whether you're chopping vegetables, stirring a pot, or simply setting the table, the mindfulness you bring to these tasks turns cooking into a sacred practice.

This chapter explores how to transform ordinary cooking into meditation, simple rituals that elevate everyday tasks, and the healing power of comfort foods. By focusing on intention and awareness, you can make every meal preparation an act of self-care and nourishment.

Transforming Ordinary Cooking into Ritual

Cooking is often thought of as a chore, but by bringing mindfulness and intention into each step, you turn even the simplest task into a sacred ritual. The key to mindful cooking lies in connecting with the present moment, grounding yourself in each action, and allowing your senses to fully experience the process.

Setting Intentions While Cooking

In Kitchen Witchery, setting intentions is a powerful way to focus your energy on a particular outcome. Whether you're seeking peace, joy, or clarity, take a moment before you begin cooking to set an intention for the meal. This could be as simple as saying, "I'm making this meal to nourish my body," or "I want to bring warmth and comfort to myself with this food." This simple act aligns your energy with your goal, infusing the food with your desired outcome.

Example of Intentional Cooking Ritual

Before chopping vegetables, take a deep breath and state your intention aloud or in your mind. As you chop, focus on that intention, allowing each slice to symbolize your commitment. Visualize the meal bringing fulfilment, health, or peace as you prepare each ingredient with love.

Speaking Affirmations Aloud: Affirmations are statements that reinforce your intentions and help focus your mind. You create a mental shift by saying positive affirmations aloud as you cook, inviting the energy you wish to bring into your life. For example, while cooking a dish to enhance self-love, you might say, "I am worthy of care and love." Repeating this affirmation aligns you with your intention, helping to infuse the meal with positive energy.

Making Everyday Tasks Sacred: Even the most mundane tasks can be turned into mindfulness rituals, making each moment in the kitchen an opportunity for magic and connection.

Chopping as a Release of Energy: When chopping ingredients, consider each cut a release of stagnant energy or stress. By focusing on the chopping rhythm, you can turn this action into a meditative practice. Each slice can represent a release of negativity, allowing you to focus on what's important.

Stirring Clockwise and Counterclockwise: In Kitchen Witchery, stirring clockwise (sunwise or Deosil) brings positive energy, helping attract the qualities you seek, like joy, abundance, or love. If you're stirring a sauce, soup, or even a bowl of batter, visualize the clockwise motion drawing in warmth, comfort, or whatever you hope the meal will provide. For balance, consider adding a few counterclockwise (Widdershins or anti-clockwise) stir to release unwanted energy.

Example: As you prepare a comforting stew, stir clockwise to bring warmth and comfort, seeing each turn as an invitation for peace and happiness.

If you're looking to release stress, add a few counterclockwise stirs, visualizing your worries melting away. Counterclockwise is also used for banishing or protecting from outside influences.

Setting the Table with Intention: Presenting food is as much a part of the ritual as cooking. When setting the table, take a moment to consider the atmosphere you're creating. Are you inviting peace, joy, or connection? Arrange each place setting thoughtfully, visualizing harmony filling the space as you place each fork, plate, and glass. Light a candle or add a sprig of herbs to the table to amplify your intention.

The Healing Power of Comfort Foods

Comfort foods hold a unique place in our lives. They often remind us of warmth, love, and moments of safety, offering physical nourishment and emotional healing. By bringing mindfulness and intention to these meals, you can amplify their comforting qualities, using them as grounding, self-care, and resilience tools.

Why Comfort Foods Bring Emotional Healing?

Comfort foods are more than just familiar flavours; they carry memories, emotions, and sensory experiences that connect us to our past. For many, a bowl of soup or a plate of mashed potatoes brings a sense of safety and warmth, often evoking memories of home, family, or happy times. This emotional response can be incredibly healing, especially during times of stress or sadness, as it provides a grounding sense of stability.

Recipes for Comforting and Nurturing Meals

These simple recipes focus on traditional comfort foods with a magical twist. They are meant to soothe the soul, ease anxiety, and provide grounding energy.

Cozy Mashed Potatoes—Grounding–Stability and Comfort

Ingredients:
- 2 large potatoes (grounding and protection)
- 2 tablespoons butter (nourishment and harmony)
- 1/4 cup milk (comfort and nurturing)
- Salt (protection)
- Fresh rosemary, chopped (clarity and mental peace)

Instructions:
1. Boil the potatoes until soft. As you peel and chop them, visualize any stress or worries melting away.
2. Mash the potatoes, adding butter and milk, setting the intention for comfort and grounding.
3. Add salt for protection and rosemary for clarity. Stir clockwise to invite stability.
4. Serve warm, focusing on each bite as an act of self-care and grounding.

Healing Vegetable Soup—Resilience–Strength and Healing

Ingredients:
- 1 tablespoon olive oil (unity and healing)
- 1 carrot, diced (fertility of ideas and success)
- 1 celery stalk, diced (clarity and connection)
- 1/2 onion, chopped (protection and courage)
- 2 garlic cloves, minced (healing and strength)

- 4 cups vegetable broth (grounding and nurturing)

- Fresh parsley (healing and vitality)

- Salt and pepper to taste

Instructions:

1. Heat the olive oil, adding carrot, celery, and onion. As they soften, focus on bringing strength and resilience into the dish.

2. Add garlic and stir, visualizing its energy infusing the soup with healing and courage.

3. Pour in the broth, stirring clockwise to amplify grounding energy.

4. Sprinkle parsley at the end, saying an affirmation for health and well-being. Enjoy the soup as a warm, healing embrace.

Sweet Honey Oat Porridge—Comfort and Love–Self-Love and Emotional Comfort

Ingredients:

- 1/2 cup rolled oats (nourishment and stability)

- 1 cup milk or almond milk (nurturing and comfort)

- 1 tablespoon honey (love and sweetness)

- A dash of cinnamon (warmth and prosperity)

- Fresh berries (protection and joy)

Instructions:

1. Cook oats in milk over medium heat, stirring with the intention of love and self-care.

2. Add honey for sweetness, stirring clockwise to invite warmth and affection.

3. Sprinkle cinnamon and top with berries, visualizing each ingredient as a gift to yourself, nourishing both body and soul.

4. Take a moment before eating to express gratitude for the meal, embracing its warmth and comfort.

Making Every Meal a Sacred Practice

Mindful cooking allows you to create moments of peace, grounding, and intention in the kitchen, transforming each meal into a sacred practice. When you approach cooking with mindfulness, even simple dishes become powerful tools for self-care, mental health, and emotional well-being. By infusing your meals with intention, choosing ingredients thoughtfully, and making every step a ritual, you're crafting food that nourishes the body and nurtures the soul. This practice reminds us that the kitchen is not just a place for cooking—it's a sanctuary for healing, meditation, and magic.

Chapter 11

RITUAL MEALS FOR EMOTIONAL HEALING

F ood has the profound power to comfort, celebrate, and heal. Through cooking, we can create rituals that provide emotional support, honour moments of joy, and bring peace during grief. Whether seeking to heal after a loss or celebrate a joyful milestone, creating intentional meals can transform cooking into a profoundly nourishing act for the soul.

This chapter explores how cooking for specific emotions, such as grief or joy, can be a form of ritualized self-care. We'll discuss the value of cooking as self-care, offer ideas for creating meaningful food rituals, and share recipes that bring comfort in sorrow and joy in celebration.

Cooking for Grief and Loss

In times of grief and loss, cooking can offer a gentle space for processing emotions. The act of preparing food can be grounding, helping you connect with the present moment and find solace in the familiar rhythm of chopping, stirring, and tasting. Foods that are warm, soft, and nurturing often bring the most comfort during periods of mourning, reminding us to take care of ourselves even when it feels difficult.

Comforting Recipes for Times of Mourning

Warm, filling foods that feel like an embrace are ideal when cooking for grief. Soups, casseroles, and stews are easy to prepare and evoke feelings of safety and warmth.

Healing Vegetable Soup—Comfort, Healing, and Peace

Ingredients:
- 1 tablespoon olive oil (healing and unity)

- 1 onion, chopped (clarity and strength)

- 2 garlic cloves, minced (protection and resilience)

- 2 carrots, diced (success and fertility of ideas)

- 2 celery stalks, diced (balance and clarity)

- 1 zucchini, diced (emotional grounding)

- 4 cups vegetable broth (nourishment and grounding)

- Fresh thyme and parsley (healing and cleansing)

- Salt and pepper to taste

Instructions:
1. Heat olive oil in a large pot over medium heat. Add onion and garlic, letting their aromas fill the kitchen and focusing on bringing in clarity and resilience.

2. Add carrots, celery, and zucchini, stirring with the intention of creating peace and comfort.

3. Pour in the broth and add thyme and parsley. Let the soup simmer gently, stirring clockwise to invite warmth and grounding.

4. Serve warm, breathing in the nourishing scents and visualizing the soup, providing comfort and healing.

Potato Casserole for Nurturing Comfort—Grounding, Protection, and Emotional Support

Ingredients:
- 3 large potatoes, sliced (grounding and stability)

- 1 cup cream or milk (nurturing and comfort)

- 1/2 cup grated cheese (nourishment)

- Fresh rosemary, finely chopped (protection and peace)

- Salt and pepper to taste

Instructions:
1. Layer the potato slices in a baking dish, focusing on the protective and grounding energy potatoes bring.

2. Pour over the cream, sprinkle cheese, and add rosemary with an intention for peace and emotional comfort.

3. Bake until golden and bubbling, letting the aroma fill your space and provide a sense of warmth and security.

4. Serve as a comforting, grounding meal to help ease the weight of grief, allowing the warmth to bring gentle solace.

Celebrating Joy Through Food

Just as food can comfort us during times of sorrow, it can also be a powerful way to celebrate moments of happiness and achievement. Cooking to mark joyful occasions—whether small milestones or major celebrations—creates memories and brings a sense of gratitude and festivity to your space. Foods that are vibrant, sweet, or rich often evoke feelings of joy, creating a sensory experience that lifts the spirit.

Recipes for Joy and Celebration

Citrus Celebration Cake—Intention: Joy, Abundance, and Celebration

Ingredients:
- 1 cup flour (abundance and growth)

- 1/2 cup sugar (sweetness and happiness)

- 1/4 cup butter, softened (comfort and warmth)

- Zest of 1 orange and 1 lemon (creativity and clarity)

- 1/2 cup orange juice (vitality and happiness)

- 1 teaspoon vanilla extract (love and clarity)

- A pinch of salt (balance)

- Powdered sugar for dusting (joy and lightness)

Instructions:
1. Preheat the oven to 350°F (175°C) and grease a baking dish (9-inch round or 8x8-inch square pan).

2. Cream the butter and sugar together, focusing on infusing the mixture with joy and warmth.

3. Add the orange and lemon zest, setting an intention for creativity and clarity, and stir in the vanilla extract.

4. Pour the batter into the dish and bake until golden, allowing the citrus aroma to fill your space with light, happy energy.

5. Once cooled, dust with powdered sugar, focusing on the sweetness of life and gratitude for the present moment.

6. This light, citrusy cake is perfect for celebrations, helping you to embrace joy and recognize your accomplishments with sweetness and gratitude.

Festive Strawberry and Basil Salad—Love, Gratitude, and Connection

Ingredients:
- 1 cup fresh strawberries, sliced (love and sweetness)

- 1/2 cup basil leaves, torn (wealth and protection)

- 1/4 cup crumbled feta cheese (nourishment)

- A drizzle of honey (harmony and attraction)

- A splash of balsamic vinegar (transformation)

Instructions:
1. In a large bowl, combine strawberries, basil, and feta. Drizzle honey and balsamic vinegar over the top.

2. Toss gently, visualizing the love, gratitude, and connection this dish will bring.

3. Serve as a refreshing, celebratory dish that embraces the sweetness of life and the joy of shared moments.

4. This salad is ideal for warm-weather celebrations, a light and refreshing reminder of life's beauty and sweetness.

If the basil is too strong for you, add only a tiny amount and replace the greens with spinach.

Infusing Food with Gratitude and Joy

Gratitude is a powerful practice that enhances our perspective and brings us back to the present moment. When we cook with gratitude, we're able to find beauty and joy in even the simplest acts, making food preparation a daily ritual of appreciation. You can incorporate gratitude into any meal by setting intentions, expressing thanks for the ingredients, or simply enjoying each step in the cooking process.

Cooking as a Form of Self-Care

Cooking is a profound act of self-care. Setting aside time to prepare meals for yourself allows you to honour your body, nourish your spirit, and enjoy the quiet ritual of creation. Self-care in the kitchen doesn't have to be elaborate—it can be as simple as a solo cooking session, a themed night, or a dedicated evening where you savour each bite.

Ideas for Self-Care Cooking

Solo Cooking Sessions: Dedicate an evening to cooking a meal just for you. Enjoy the process without distractions, perhaps with soft music or a favourite podcast in the background. Focus on chopping, stirring, and creating rhythms, finding comfort in these mindful actions.

Themed Cooking Nights: Choose a theme that resonates with your needs, such as "Comfort Food" or "International Cuisine." This can be an opportunity to experiment, unwind, and enjoy the process of exploring new flavours.

Mindful Eating: Once your meal is ready, sit down with intention. Turn off distractions, focus on the flavours and textures, and let each bite remind you of the nourishment you've created for yourself.

Creating Rituals Around Food

Rituals bring structure, meaning, and comfort to everyday activities. Adding rituals to your cooking and dining practice turns mealtime into a sacred experience, a moment to express gratitude, celebrate milestones, or honour the present.

Gratitude Practice

Before each meal, express gratitude for the food on your plate, the hands that prepared it, and the nourishment it provides. Taking a moment of gratitude before eating helps cultivate an abundant mindset, reminding you to appreciate the small gifts in life.

Celebration of Milestones

Food is a powerful way to mark achievements and milestones. Whether it's a new job, a birthday, or a personal accomplishment, celebrating with a special meal honours these moments. Create a dish you love, gather with friends or family, and use food to recognize the progress in your journey.

Honouring Your Emotions Through Food

Whether it's cooking to soothe a grieving heart, celebrating with joyful dishes, or using food as a form of self-care, the kitchen is a place where emotions can be honoured and transformed. Cooking offers a way to express and process feelings, mark milestones, and connect with ourselves and others. By bringing ritual and mindfulness into your cooking practice, each meal becomes a way to heal, celebrate, and find peace. In these small but significant acts, food becomes more than sustenance—it becomes a nourishing force for emotional well-being and growth.

Chapter 12

SEASONAL KITCHEN MAGIC

C ooking with the rhythm of the seasons connects us to the natural world, enhancing our culinary practice and fostering a deeper awareness of nature's cycles. Each season brings a unique bounty of ingredients and invites different energies into the kitchen. By aligning your cooking with the Wheel of the Year, you can infuse each meal with intention, celebrating renewal, abundance, gratitude, and reflection as the year unfolds.

This chapter explores seasonal kitchen magic, including ingredients, recipes, and rituals to celebrate each season. From spring's fresh greens to winter's hearty stews, we'll discover how to use the magic of the seasons to nourish both body and spirit.

The Wheel of the Year and Seasonal Recipes

The Wheel of the Year marks the passage of time through nature's cycles, with each season offering its own magical energy. Seasonal cooking allows you to embrace the spirit of each season, using ingredients that reflect its essence. By focusing on what's fresh and available, you can create meals that honour the natural world while enhancing your well-being.

Spring: Renewal and Fresh Beginnings

As winter gives way to spring, the world comes alive with new growth and vibrant energy. This season is associated with renewal, growth, and fresh starts, making it a perfect time to focus on light, herb-focused meals that symbolize new beginnings. Fresh greens, sprouts, and tender herbs are ideal for spring dishes, bringing revitalizing energy to the table.

Ingredients for Spring Magic

Peas: Symbolize prosperity and renewal, perfect for bringing fresh energy into your meals.

Asparagus: Associated with fertility and growth, ideal for setting intentions for new projects or personal development.

Mint: Fresh and cooling, mint brings clarity and focus, helping you embrace the freshness of spring.

Spring Herb and Pea Salad—Renewal and Growth

Ingredients:

- 1 cup fresh peas (prosperity and renewal)

- 1/2 cup chopped asparagus (growth and fertility)

- A handful of fresh mint leaves, chopped (clarity)

- 1/4 cup crumbled feta cheese (nourishment)

- Olive oil and lemon juice for dressing (vitality and purification)

Instructions:

1. In a large bowl, combine the peas, asparagus, and mint.

2. Drizzle with olive oil and lemon juice, and toss gently.

3. Add feta cheese, setting an intention for growth and renewal with each ingredient.

4. Enjoy this light salad, savouring the fresh flavours as a celebration of spring's renewal.

Summer: Vibrancy and Abundance

Summer is a season of abundance, warmth, and celebration. With nature in full bloom, it's the perfect time to embrace bright, colourful fruits and vegetables. This season encourages us to celebrate life's richness, so focus on vibrant, joyful dishes that reflect the fullness of summer.

Ingredients for Summer Magic

Tomatoes: Represent love and vitality, bringing warmth and brightness to dishes.

Berries: Symbolize joy and sweetness, perfect for celebrating happiness and love.

Basil: Known for wealth and protection, basil adds a burst of flavor and magic to summer meals.

Heirloom Tomato and Basil Pasta—Abundance and Joy

Ingredients:

- 1 cup cooked pasta (abundance and growth)

- 1 cup chopped heirloom tomatoes (love and vitality)

- 1/4 cup fresh basil leaves, torn (wealth and protection)

- 1 tablespoon olive oil (unity and healing)

- Salt and pepper to taste

Instructions:

1. In a large bowl, combine the pasta, tomatoes, and basil.

2. Drizzle with olive oil and toss, visualizing the energy of summer's abundance filling each bite.

3. Sprinkle with salt and pepper, focusing on joy and gratitude for the season's bounty.

4. Serve and enjoy as a celebration of summer's vibrant energy.

Autumn: Harvest and Gratitude

Autumn brings a season of harvest, reflection, and gratitude. It's a time to savor the fruits of the earth and prepare for the coming winter. Root vegetables, pumpkins, and apples are abundant, offering warmth and nourishment. Autumn dishes are hearty and grounding, perfect for sharing with loved ones and expressing thanks for nature's abundance.

Ingredients for Autumn Magic

Pumpkins: Represent prosperity and protection, ideal for grounding and stability.

Apples: Symbolize love and wisdom, bringing warmth to dishes.

Sage: Known for wisdom and protection, sage adds a grounding quality to autumn meals.

Harvest Pumpkin and Sage Soup—Gratitude and Grounding

Ingredients:
- 2 cups pumpkin puree (prosperity and protection)

- 1 onion, chopped (clarity and courage)

- 2 garlic cloves, minced (healing and strength)

- 1 tablespoon fresh sage, chopped (wisdom and grounding)

- 4 cups vegetable broth (nourishment)

- Salt and pepper to taste

Instructions:

1. In a pot, sauté the onion and garlic until soft, setting the intention for clarity and strength.

2. Add pumpkin puree, sage, and vegetable broth, stirring clockwise to attract grounding energy.

3. Let the soup simmer, filling the kitchen with warm, comforting aromas. Focus on gratitude for the season's abundance.

4. Serve warm, sharing with loved ones or enjoying as a ritual of thanks.

Winter: Reflection and Warmth

Winter is a season of introspection, rest, and gathering. As the world slows down, we're drawn to cozy, hearty meals that bring warmth and comfort. Grains, legumes, and root vegetables are ideal winter ingredients, creating nourishing dishes that support rest and reflection. Winter dishes often involve slow cooking, encouraging patience and mindfulness.

Ingredients for Winter Magic

Potatoes: Symbolize grounding and stability, perfect for winter's introspective energy.

Carrots: Associated with resilience and strength, adding a touch of warmth to meals.

Rosemary: Known for clarity and protection, rosemary brings a comforting energy to winter dishes.

Cozy Rosemary and Root Vegetable Stew—Reflection and Comfort

Ingredients:

- 2 large potatoes, diced (grounding and protection)

- 2 carrots, sliced (strength and resilience)

- 1 onion, chopped (clarity and courage)

- 2 garlic cloves, minced (protection and healing)

- 1 tablespoon fresh rosemary, chopped (clarity and comfort)

- 4 cups vegetable broth (nourishment)

- Salt and pepper to taste

Instructions:

1. In a large pot, sauté onion and garlic, infusing the stew with protection and warmth.

2. Add potatoes, carrots, rosemary, and broth, stirring clockwise, with an intention for comfort and reflection.

3. Let the stew simmer, filling your kitchen with its hearty aroma. Then, reflect on the past year and give thanks for the lessons learned.

4. Serve warm, allowing each spoonful to nourish and ground you during winter's quiet season.

Seasonal Cooking and Rituals

Aligning your cooking with the seasons deepens your connection to nature's cycles. Seasonal ingredients carry the energy of the time of year, and using them mindfully can enhance your culinary magic. Seasonal cooking isn't just about flavour; it's about engaging with the earth's rhythm and finding harmony with the changing world.

Spring Ritual: When cooking with fresh herbs and greens, visualize new beginnings. Let each ingredient embody the spirit of renewal and growth.

Summer Ritual: Embrace the warmth and energy of summer by choosing vibrant, colourful foods. Visualize joy and celebration as you chop, stir, and create.

Autumn Ritual: As you prepare hearty autumn meals, reflect on what you are grateful for, honouring the abundance in your life.

Winter Ritual: In winter, slow-cooked meals allow you to meditate and reflect. Set an intention for warmth and comfort, letting each step of the process bring you closer to stillness.

Seasonal Feasts and Celebrations

Seasonal gatherings bring people together to celebrate the cycles of the year, connecting us to nature and to each other. Hosting a seasonal feast can be a meaningful way to honour the changing seasons and share gratitude with loved ones.

Harvest Celebration: Organize a fall gathering to celebrate the harvest season. Prepare dishes with pumpkins, squash, and apples, and encourage guests to share what they're grateful for.

Solstice and Equinox Dinners: Mark the solstices and equinoxes with special meals that reflect the energies of each season. Consider bright and colourful dishes for a summer solstice, while a winter solstice feast might focus on warmth and comfort.

Seasonal Decor: Add seasonal elements to your kitchen, like fresh flowers in spring, autumn leaves, or winter greenery. These small touches create an inspiring environment and keep you attuned to nature's rhythms.

Cooking with the Seasons

Seasonal kitchen magic is a practice that invites you to align with the natural world, connecting each meal with the energies of renewal, abundance, gratitude, and introspection. By choosing seasonal ingredients, creating rituals around your cooking, and celebrating nature's cycles, you bring a deeper meaning to every meal. Embrace the Wheel of the Year as your guide, letting each season inspire and ground you in the sacred cooking practice with intention.

Chapter 13

SIMPLE RECIPES FOR MIND, BODY, AND SPIRIT

Cooking for mind, body, and spirit can be a transformative practice that nurtures both physical and emotional well-being. By preparing food with intention, choosing ingredients mindfully, and engaging in the process of intuitive cooking, you can create meals that go beyond sustenance to support self-care, manifestation, and personal growth. This chapter offers simple recipes, encourages intuitive and creative cooking, and provides tips on meal planning with purpose.

Recipes for Self-Care

Self-care in the kitchen can be as simple as preparing a warm, nourishing meal or a comforting cup of tea. These recipes are designed to offer grounding energy, comfort, and support for both mind and body.

Nourishing Broth—Peace and Healing

A warm, simple broth can be a balm for the soul, offering comfort during times of stress or exhaustion. This broth is rich in grounding ingredients and infused with healing herbs to restore balance and peace.

Ingredients:

- 1 tablespoon olive oil (unity and healing)

- 1 onion, chopped (clarity and strength)

- 2 carrots, sliced (nourishment and resilience)

- 2 celery stalks, chopped (balance and focus)

- 4 cups vegetable or bone broth (grounding and protection)

- Fresh rosemary and thyme sprigs (clarity and strength)

- Salt and pepper to taste

Instructions:

1. Heat olive oil in a pot and add onion, carrots, and celery. Sauté until soft, visualizing warmth and peace.

2. Pour in the broth and add rosemary and thyme. Let the broth simmer, infusing the herbs' energy.

3. Serve warm, allowing each sip to bring comfort and calm.

Rosemary Biscuits—Grounding and Clarity

This simple bread recipe combines flour's grounding energy with rosemary's clarity-enhancing properties. Ideal for grounding yourself, rosemary bread can be enjoyed on its own or as an accompaniment to soups and stews.

Ingredients:

- 2 cups flour (abundance and grounding)

- 1 tablespoon fresh rosemary, chopped (clarity and protection)

- 1 – 1.5 teaspoons of baking powder

- 1 teaspoon salt (purification)

- 1 tablespoon olive oil (healing and unity)

- 3/4 cup water (flexibility and flow)

Instructions:

1. Mix flour, rosemary, baking soda, and salt in a bowl. Add olive oil and water, kneading until a dough forms.

2. Shape the dough into 6-8 biscuits

3. Bake at 425°F (220°C) for 12-15 minutes until the tops are golden and the biscuits feel firm to the touch. Enjoy the biscuits with a focus on centring and calming energy.

Recipes for Manifestation and Growth

Cooking with intention can support your goals and dreams, and these recipes are aligned with themes of manifestation and growth. You can infuse your meals with purpose by selecting ingredients and recipes that symbolize progress, transformation, and abundance.

Pasta With Tomatoes—Progress and Forward Momentum

Pasta is often associated with progress, thanks to its long strands symbolizing continuity and direction. This light and flavourful pasta dish combines fresh vegetables for energy and basil for abundance.

Ingredients:

- 1 cup pasta (progress and growth)

- 1/2 cup cherry tomatoes, halved (love and vitality)

- 1/4 cup fresh basil leaves, torn (prosperity and abundance)

- 2 tablespoons olive oil (healing and unity)

- Salt and pepper to taste

Instructions:

1. Cook pasta according to package instructions. Drain and set aside.

2. In a pan, heat olive oil, add tomatoes, and sauté until soft.

3. Toss in the pasta and basil, stirring clockwise to invite progress and growth.

4. Serve with gratitude, visualizing forward momentum with each bite.

Spicy Curry—Transformation and Empowerment

Curries, with their complex flavours and warming spices, symbolize transformation and empowerment. This dish is ideal when you're working toward change or embracing a new phase in life.

Ingredients:

- 1 tablespoon coconut oil (protection and balance)

- 1 onion, diced (clarity and strength)

- 1 bell pepper, diced (energy and creativity)

- 2 garlic cloves, minced (protection and resilience)

- 1 tablespoon curry powder (transformation and courage)

- 1 can coconut milk (nurturing and comfort)

- Fresh cilantro for garnish (healing and cleansing)

- Salt and pepper to taste

Instructions:

1. Heat coconut oil in a pan and add onion, bell pepper, and garlic, focusing on resilience and transformation. Cook until soft.

2. Stir in the curry powder, coating the ingredients with the intention of change.

3. Add coconut milk, simmer, and let the flavours meld, visualizing empowerment and growth.

4. Garnish with cilantro, serving the dish with gratitude for the courage to

embrace transformation.

Intuitive Cooking

Intuitive cooking is a practice that encourages you to listen to your instincts and allows your creativity to guide your choices. By letting go of strict recipes and cooking with your senses, you create meals that reflect how you feel in the moment, leading to unique, nourishing dishes.

Cooking Without Recipes

Try cooking without a strict recipe. Start by gathering ingredients that appeal to you or align with your intentions for the day. Let your senses guide you—feel the textures, smell the aromas, and taste as you go. This can lead to unexpected flavour combinations and a deeper connection to your creativity.

Example: Begin by choosing a base, such as pasta, rice, or grains. Add vegetables, proteins, and herbs as you feel drawn to them. Perhaps a sprinkle of rosemary for clarity or a handful of spinach for growth. Let your intuition take the lead and create a dish that truly reflects your intentions and desires.

Sensory Exploration

Engaging all your senses in cooking makes the process more immersive and fulfilling. Pay attention to colours, textures, and aromas, allowing these sensory experiences to guide your cooking decisions.

Exercise: As you cook, notice the vivid colour of the ingredients, the sound of simmering, and the aroma of spices. Allow these experiences to inform your next steps, making adjustments based on what feels right rather than sticking to a fixed plan.

Creating Signature Dishes

Creating a signature dish is a way to express your personality and style in the kitchen. These dishes can become your personal symbols of magic and intention, unique to your own taste and meaning.

Experimenting with Flavours

Experiment with different flavour profiles and techniques to create dishes that resonate with you. Play with spices, herbs, and textures, letting your taste preferences guide your choices. This process is playful and empowering, allowing you to explore what feels authentic.

Example: If you enjoy bold flavours, create a signature dish with spicy elements like chilli peppers balanced with grounding herbs like thyme. Or, if you prefer comfort foods, focus on creamy, nourishing ingredients that evoke warmth and care.

Personal Touch

Infuse your signature dishes with personal meaning. Perhaps you use a specific ingredient that reminds you of a loved one or incorporate a cooking technique passed down in your family. These personal touches enhance the magic of the dish, turning it into a ritual of self-expression and connection.

The Power of Meal Planning

Meal planning can be an intentional way to bring kitchen witchery into your daily routine. By planning your meals around specific intentions, you make space for creativity, mindfulness, and self-care.

Weekly Themes

Assign themes to each week's meals to inspire creativity and encourage exploration. Themes like "Meatless Mondays," "Wellness Wednesdays," or "Comfort Food Fridays" can guide your ingredient choices and align with specific intentions.

Example: For a Wellness Wednesday, plan nourishing meals filled with vegetables, grains, and healing herbs like ginger or turmeric. This focus on wellness encourages mindful choices and supports your body's needs.

Intentional Grocery Shopping

Be mindful as you shop for ingredients, choosing foods that align with your goals and desires for the week. Whether you're looking for comfort, nourishment, or celebration, consciously selecting ingredients enhances the energy of your cooking and strengthens your intentions.

Example: As you shop, pause to consider each ingredient. Select vegetables for grounding, herbs for clarity, or grains for abundance; choosing foods that reflect your intentions and support your well-being.

Cooking as a Ritual for Mind, Body, and Spirit

Integrating simple, intentional recipes with practices like intuitive cooking, signature dishes, and meal planning transforms cooking into a holistic ritual that nourishes the mind, body, and spirit. Each dish becomes a form of self-care, a tool for manifestation, and a way to express your unique energy.

As you cook, let intuition and intention guide you. Whether you're preparing nourishing broths, experimenting with flavours, or thoughtfully planning meals, each act of cooking can be a celebration of creativity, nourishment, and connection to your inner self. Embrace this journey in the kitchen as a path to wholeness, making each meal a sacred offering to your own growth and well-being.

Chapter 14

INTENTIONAL RITUALS TO ALIGN WITH YOUR NEEDS

C reating intentional rituals around food can be a powerful way to align with your needs, whether you're looking for clarity in the morning or peace in the evening. Kitchen witchery offers countless ways to incorporate intention into your daily routines, transforming meals into nourishing rituals that support your mind, body, and spirit. This chapter explores how to set the tone for your day with morning rituals, wind down in the evening with soothing meals, and continue your journey with kitchen magic as a personal practice.

Morning Rituals: Starting the Day with Intention

Morning rituals provide an opportunity to start each day with clarity, purpose, and calm. By preparing breakfast mindfully and choosing teas or foods that support focus and peace, you can set an intentional foundation for the day ahead.

Herbal Teas for Clarity and Calm

Starting your day with an herbal tea can help you feel centred and energized. Different herbs carry unique properties that can align with your intentions for the morning.

Mint Tea: Mint is known for its uplifting and clarifying properties, perfect for a fresh start. Brew a cup of mint tea while setting an intention for mental clarity and focus.

Lemon Balm Tea: Lemon balm promotes calm and peace, making it ideal for days when you're looking to stay grounded. Sip a warm cup in the morning, visualizing a calm, balanced day ahead.

Green Tea with Basil: Combining green tea's energizing qualities with basil's abundance properties can help bring a sense of purpose and vitality to your morning.

Breakfast Ideas for Focus and Energy

Breakfast can be a grounding ritual that nourishes the body and clears the mind. Choose ingredients that promote clarity, energy, and calm, and focus on eating slowly and mindfully.

Oatmeal with Berries and Honey—Grounding, Joy, and Sweetness

Ingredients:
- 1/2 cup quick oats (stability and grounding)

- 1/2 cup milk or plant milk (comfort)

- A handful of berries (joy and protection)

- 1 teaspoon honey (love and sweetness)

Instructions:
1. Prepare the oatmeal by simmering the oats in milk until soft.

2. Top with berries and drizzle honey, focusing on grounding and sweetness for the day ahead.

3. Enjoy each bite mindfully, envisioning a day filled with joy, focus, and gratitude.

Avocado Toast with Fresh Herbs—Clarity, Health, and Fresh Beginnings

Ingredients:

- 1 slice whole-grain bread (abundance)

- 1/2 avocado, mashed (prosperity and health)

- Fresh parsley or basil, chopped (clarity and vitality)

- Poached or soft cooked egg – over-easy, sunny-side-up (new beginnings)

- A sprinkle of sea salt (protection)

Instructions:

1. Lightly toast the bread.

2. Spread the mashed avocado on toast, adding a sprinkle of herbs for clarity.

3. Place the egg on top of the avocado mixture.

4. Set an intention for fresh beginnings and clarity, visualizing the energy of health and vitality.

5. Savour each bite, feeling grounded and ready for the day.

Evening Rituals: Ending the Day with Peace

Evening rituals allow you to reflect on the day, unwind, and transition to a state of relaxation. By creating comforting, stress-relieving meals in the evening, you can prepare your body and mind for rest.

Recipes for Relaxing Dinners

End your day with a meal that provides warmth and comfort, incorporating ingredients known for their calming and grounding properties.

Soothing Vegetable Soup with Sage—Relaxation, Reflection, and Grounding

Ingredients:

- 1 tablespoon olive oil (unity and healing)

- 1 onion, diced (clarity and strength)

- 2 carrots, sliced (nourishment and resilience)

- 1 celery stalk, chopped (balance)

- 4 cups vegetable broth (grounding)

- Fresh sage, chopped (wisdom and calm)

Instructions:

1. Sauté onion, carrots, and celery in olive oil, focusing on grounding and reflection.

2. Add broth and sage, letting the soup simmer while setting an intention for relaxation.

3. Serve warm, allowing each spoonful to ease your mind and bring you peace.

Comforting Garlic Mashed Potatoes—Comfort, Self-Love, and Release

Ingredients:

- 3 large potatoes, peeled and diced (grounding)

- 1/4 cup milk or cream (nurturing)

- 2 cloves garlic, minced (protection)

- 1 tablespoon butter (warmth and love)

Instructions:

1. Boil potatoes until tender, mashing them with milk, garlic, and butter.

2. Visualize releasing any stress or worries from the day as you stir, welcoming comfort and self-love.

3. Enjoy the warmth and softness of the dish, allowing it to bring a sense of relaxation and care.

Using Food to Wind Down and Reflect

As you enjoy your evening meal, take a moment to breathe deeply, grounding yourself in the present. This time of reflection can help you process the day's experiences and let go of any lingering stress. Express gratitude for the meal, the hands that prepared it, and the nourishment it provides, allowing you to end your day with a sense of fulfilment.

Exploring Recipes with Intentions

Infusing meals with intentions is a powerful way to align cooking with your emotional and spiritual needs. Throughout your kitchen witchery journey, you can experiment with different dishes that embody principles of healing, manifestation, and growth.

Nourishing Herbal Broth—Health and Vitality

A simple herbal broth can serve as a nurturing ritual for health and vitality. Use healing herbs like thyme and ginger, focusing on self-care and well-being as you prepare it.

Ingredients:

- 1 tablespoon olive oil (unity)

- 1 onion, chopped (clarity)

- Fresh thyme and ginger (healing)

- 4 cups vegetable broth (grounding)

Instructions:

1. Sauté the onion, adding thyme and ginger with intention.

2. Pour in the broth and let simmer, visualizing health and vitality with each stir.

3. Sip slowly, focusing on the warmth and nourishment.

GOOD MORNING
Simple Avocado Toast with Fresh Herbs

Affirmation

"With each bite, I welcome clarity, health, and abundance into my life. I am nourished, grounded, and ready for new beginnings today."

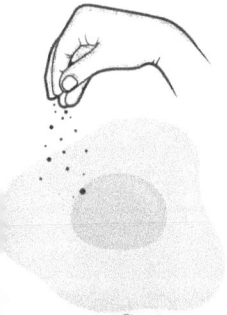

Pinch of Salt

Fried Egg

Parsley

1/2 Mashed Avocado

Toast

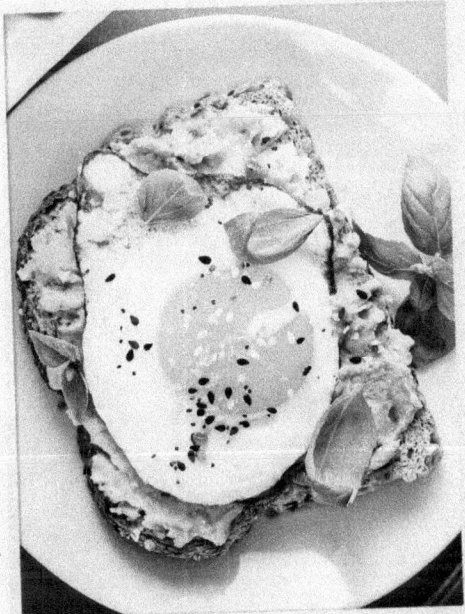

Part 3

COMMUNITY, CONNECTION, AND KITCHEN WITCHERY

Chapter 15

THE MAGIC OF SHARING FOOD

S haring food is a powerful way to connect, build relationships, and foster community. In Kitchen Witchery, the act of preparing and sharing a meal goes beyond nourishment; it becomes a ritual of bonding, healing, and love. Whether you're gathering with friends, bringing food to a potluck, or preparing a meal for someone in need, sharing food can strengthen bonds, offer support, and create lasting memories.

This chapter explores the magic of sharing food, from potluck rituals to cooking as an act of love. We'll look at how food can foster connections and offer comfort and explore the ethical considerations of cooking for others with intention and care.

Using Food to Strengthen Bonds

Food has an incredible way of bringing people together. A shared meal can bridge differences, deepen friendships, and create a sense of belonging. When you prepare food with the intention of fostering connection, each ingredient and action carries that energy, enhancing the experience for everyone involved.

Potluck Rituals: Building Community Through Shared Meals

Potlucks are wonderful gatherings that allow everyone to contribute to a shared meal, creating diverse flavours and energies. A potluck brings together different dishes, stories, and experiences, symbolizing the beauty of community and shared contribution.

Potluck Ritual Ideas

Setting Intentions Together: Before the meal begins, gather with everyone to set a shared intention for the evening. This could be a theme, such as "gratitude" or "joy." Each person can briefly share what their dish represents or what energy they infused into it.

Gratitude Circle: As everyone is seated, go around the table and express gratitude. This could be for the food, the people gathered, or simply the opportunity to come together. A gratitude circle fosters a feeling of abundance and connection, amplifying the positive energy in the room.

Creating a Potluck Altar: Arrange a small space with candles, flowers, or meaningful objects to honour the gathering. Place each dish near the altar as a symbolic offering to the shared intention of the meal.

Potlucks offer a beautiful way to contribute to community spirit and create a space where everyone feels included and valued. With each person bringing a dish, the meal becomes a collaborative expression of care and connection.

Ritualized Meal-Sharing for Connection and Support

Sharing a meal with loved ones can be a profound act of connection. The ritual of sitting down together, passing dishes, and engaging in conversation strengthens bonds and offers support. When shared mindfully, a meal becomes a sacred space for sharing feelings, expressing gratitude, and nurturing one another.

Rituals to Deepen Connection During Meals

Silent Reflection: Begin the meal with a moment of silent reflection. Each person can take a deep breath, focus on their intentions, and connect with the energy of the group.

Pass the Dish Ritual: As you pass dishes around the table, imagine each person adding a bit of positive energy—such as love, peace, or support. This creates a circle of energy that surrounds everyone at the table.

Shared Blessing: Before eating, offer a simple blessing together. This can be a line of gratitude or an affirmation, like "May this meal bring us closer in heart and spirit."

Creating these small rituals around shared meals fosters a sense of unity and belonging. They allow each person to feel valued and included, making the meal a memorable and meaningful experience.

Cooking for Others as an Act of Love

One of the most powerful ways to express care and support is by cooking for others. Whether you're making a meal for a loved one, a friend in need, or a neighbour, the act of preparing food with love and intention becomes a powerful form of healing. Cooking for others is a gift of time, energy, and warmth, showing that they are valued and cherished.

Healing Recipes for Comfort and Support

Meals prepared for healing and comfort often focus on warmth, nourishment, and simplicity. Here are a few recipes with intentions that offer comfort, support, and healing energy to those who receive them.

Heartwarming Chicken Soup—Healing and Comfort

Ingredients:
- 1 tablespoon olive oil (unity and healing)

- 1 onion, diced (clarity and courage)

- 2 carrots, sliced (nourishment and resilience)

- 2 celery stalks, sliced (clarity and connection)

- 2 garlic cloves, minced (protection and strength)

- 4 cups chicken broth (grounding and comfort)

- 1 bay leaf (peace and wisdom)

- Fresh parsley, chopped (healing and vitality)

- Salt and pepper to taste

Instructions:

1. Heat olive oil in a large pot over medium heat. Add onion, carrots, celery, and garlic, focusing on the intention of healing and warmth.

2. Pour in the broth, add the bay leaf, and let simmer until vegetables are tender.

3. Stir in parsley, visualizing comfort and healing as you finish the soup.

4. Serve warm to offer comfort and support, or package it to deliver as a thoughtful, nourishing gift.

Creamy Mashed Potatoes—Grounding and Emotional Support

Ingredients:

- 4 large potatoes, peeled and diced (grounding and stability)

- 1/2 cup milk (nurturing and comfort)

- 1/4 cup butter (warmth and harmony)

- Salt and pepper to taste

Instructions:

1. Boil the potatoes until soft. As you peel and dice them, focus on ground-

ing and stability.

2. Mash the potatoes with milk and butter, setting the intention for emotional support and care.

3. Serve or share as a comforting dish that brings warmth and peace.

Sweet Honey Oat Cookies—Love and Joy

Ingredients:
- 1 cup rolled oats (nourishment and grounding)

- 1/2 cup flour (abundance and growth)

- 1/4 cup honey (harmony and sweetness)

- 1/4 cup butter, softened (comfort and love)

- A pinch of cinnamon (warmth and joy)

Instructions:
1. Mix oats, flour, honey, and butter, visualizing love and joy with each stir.

2. Add a pinch of cinnamon to bring warmth to the cookies.

3. Bake until golden and share with someone as a reminder of joy and sweetness in life.

4. These recipes are intended to offer comfort, support, and connection, transforming cooking into an act of love and care.

Ethical Considerations: Consent and Intention When Cooking for Others

When cooking for others, it's essential to approach the act with respect, consent, and consideration. Cooking with intention can be powerful, but it's important to ensure that the recipient is open to receiving the energy and intention behind the meal.

Consent: Always make sure that the person is comfortable receiving food, especially if it's infused with specific intentions or energy. Some people may have dietary restrictions, allergies, or personal preferences that must be respected.

Intention: Keep your intentions positive and open when cooking for others. While it's natural to want to help, be mindful that each person has their own journey and needs. Rather than imposing specific intentions, offer support, comfort, and healing energy, allowing the recipient to accept it in their own way.

Transparency: If you're infusing the food with particular energies or intentions, consider sharing this with the recipient in a gentle way. This can foster mutual understanding and respect for your practice.

By cooking with integrity, respect, and mindfulness, you ensure that your food becomes a genuine expression of love and support.

Embracing the Magic of Shared Food

The magic of sharing food lies in its ability to foster connection, offer comfort and strengthen bonds. Through potluck rituals, shared meals, and thoughtful dishes prepared with love, food becomes a means of creating community and nurturing relationships. Cooking for others is a powerful act of love, filled with the energy and intention of care and support.

By bringing mindfulness to the act of sharing food, you make each meal a meaningful ritual, enriching both your life and the lives of those around you. Whether it's a gathering of friends or a simple meal prepared for a loved one, shared food nourishes not only the body but the heart and soul.

Chapter 16

COOKING TOGETHER AS COLLECTIVE HEALING

C ollaborative cooking rituals are a powerful way to bring people together, foster community, and infuse meals with meaningful intentions. When we cook together, each person contributes a unique energy and perspective, transforming the act of preparing food into a shared ritual of support, celebration, and healing. From honouring family traditions to preparing comfort meals for those in need, collaborative cooking builds bonds that nourish both body and soul.

This chapter explores a variety of collaborative cooking rituals, each designed to bring people together with a shared purpose. Whether you're making a comforting meal for someone in mourning, celebrating a birthday, or preserving seasonal fruits, these rituals emphasize the magic of community, tradition, and mutual support.

Stone Soup Ritual: A Meal for Community Support

The idea of "Stone Soup" stems from a folk tale where travellers arrive in a village with nothing but a pot and a stone. They start a soup, and one by one, villagers contribute ingredients, transforming it into a hearty meal for all. This collaborative dish symbolizes the magic that happens when everyone brings something to the table, creating abundance from shared effort.

Event: Organize a Stone Soup-style gathering where each person brings an ingredient to contribute to a communal soup or stew.

Magical Aspect: As each person adds their ingredient, they can focus on an intention, such as gratitude, love, or abundance. Participants can say aloud (or silently) what they are contributing to the collective energy of the meal.

Mental Health Focus: Discuss the importance of community support and how sharing food can ease loneliness or isolation. Encourage participants to reflect on the value of connection and mutual care as they cook and eat together.

Preparing a Healing Meal for Someone Who Lost a Loved One

This section could cover two different scenarios, cooking a mean for someone in mourning, but also cooking with someone who is in mourning. Depending on the person and stage of grief, yours and theirs.

Cooking For Someone in Mourning

This could be done as an individual or as a group. Unfortunately, we will all experience loss or have someone we care about experience loss. It can be challenging to know what to do to provide support. From my own experience, I recall friends and family asking, "What can I do?" or "Let me know what I can do to help." That put all the pressure on me to find something for them to do so they feel better. However, other people just showed up with a meal that went in the fridge or freezer or that extraordinary friend who cleaned the house knowing people would be coming over.

The meals can be helpful in ensuring people eat when they feel motivated to, as well as in serving food when well-meaning friends or family stay longer than expected.

Cooking With Someone in Mourning

Cooking for someone in mourning can be an act of profound compassion. Preparing a comforting meal as a group can provide emotional support, allowing the bereaved person to feel surrounded by love and care during a difficult time.

Event: Host a gathering where each participant contributes to making a hearty soup, casserole, or another comforting dish for someone in mourning.

Magical Aspect: As each person adds their ingredients, they can set an intention for healing, comfort, and peace. Participants may share memories of the loved one if they knew them, or simply offer words of support and love, imbuing the meal with healing energy.

Mental Health Focus: Encourage participants to share memories and positive thoughts, honouring the spirit of the loved one through shared storytelling. Create a safe place to share without judgement. It is okay to laugh remembering something about someone who has passed.

Birthday Dinner Celebration

Celebrating a birthday with a collaborative cooking ritual emphasizes the importance of honouring personal milestones and strengthening connections. Cooking together creates a joyful atmosphere where everyone contributes to making the day special.

Event: Organize a birthday dinner where friends gather to cook the birthday person's favourite dishes or a meal that aligns with their personality and preferences.

Magical Aspect: Begin the meal with a blessing ritual, where each participant shares their wishes or intentions for the birthday person in the coming year. This collective focus amplifies positive energy, filling the meal with love and support.

Mental Health Focus: Emphasize the value of celebrating personal milestones and the positive impact of community on mental well-being. Laughter, shared stories, and joy foster a strong sense of connection, making the birthday person feel loved and appreciated.

Meal Prepping and Freezing Together

Meal prepping as a group is both practical and empowering. Coming together to prepare meals for busy days ahead fosters a sense of productivity and self-care, while creating space for community and connection.

Event: Host a meal prep day where everyone gathers to cook and freeze dishes for future use. Each participant can make a batch of a favourite recipe, sharing a portion with others to enjoy later.

Magical Aspect: As each dish is prepared, participants can set intentions for health, nourishment, or abundance. Use protective or healing herbs like basil, rosemary, or thyme to enhance the magical energy of the food.

Mental Health Focus: Discuss the benefits of meal prepping for reducing stress and promoting self-care. Encourage participants to reflect on their goals for health and well-being, focusing on how prepared meals can support them in staying nourished during busy times.

Making Preserves or Jams

Gathering to make preserves or jams from seasonal fruits is a lovely way to celebrate the harvest and create something that can be enjoyed throughout the year. This ritual is perfect for autumn, when fruits like apples and berries are in abundance.

Event: Host a gathering where participants come together to make preserves or jams using seasonal ingredients.

Magical Aspect: Encourage participants to infuse each jar with positive intentions, such as abundance, sweetness in life, or a sense of preservation. Adding herbs like mint for clarity or basil for prosperity can enhance the magical properties of the preserves.

Mental Health Focus: Discuss the act of preservation as a metaphor for holding onto positive memories and experiences. Encourage participants to share stories or memories associated with the fruits they're using, creating a sense of connection and nostalgia.

Fermentation Workshop

Fermentation is a transformative process, turning basic ingredients into flavourful, nutritious foods. This workshop offers a hands-on way to engage with the metaphor of transformation, making it perfect for times of personal growth or change.

Event: Host a fermentation workshop where participants learn to make fermented foods, like kimchi, sauerkraut, or pickles.

Magical Aspect: Discuss the transformative power of fermentation as a metaphor for personal growth. As participants prepare their fermentation jars, they can set intentions for what they want to cultivate or transform in their lives.

Mental Health Focus: Highlight the benefits of fermented foods for gut health and overall well-being. Encourage participants to reflect on how nurturing the body can positively impact mental health, reinforcing the connection between physical and emotional care.

Comfort Food Cooking Class

Comfort food holds a unique place in our hearts, often tied to childhood memories, family traditions, or moments of solace. A comfort food cooking class allows participants to explore these associations and create meals that bring emotional warmth and security.

Event: Organize a cooking class focused on creating classic comfort foods, like mac and cheese, mashed potatoes, or hearty soups.

Magical Aspect: Encourage participants to select ingredients based on their personal associations with comfort, security, or joy. Each participant can share a story about the dish they chose, creating a space for connection and shared nostalgia.

Mental Health Focus: Discuss the role of comfort food in emotional well-being and the importance of self-care. Create an environment that fosters openness, allowing participants to connect and support each other through shared stories and culinary experiences.

Food, Family, and Ancestral Magic

Family recipes carry a powerful energy, linking us to our ancestors and preserving cultural wisdom. Cooking these recipes honours family traditions, allowing us to connect with inherited wisdom and ancestral energy.

Honouring Family Traditions and Recipes

Cooking family recipes or meals that were loved by those who came before us creates a tangible link to our ancestry. Whether it's a traditional holiday dish or a simple family favourite, these meals can bring a comforting sense of belonging and continuity.

Ways to Honour Ancestral Magic Through Cooking

Reviving Family Recipes: Prepare a dish passed down through generations, focusing on the memories and stories associated with it. This can be a way to honour your family's history and the love that went into each recipe.

Creating a Family Recipe Book: Gather family recipes and document them in a book, adding notes on their origins, special memories, or family traditions. This can be a cherished heirloom that preserves your family's culinary legacy.

Cooking with Inherited Tools: Use kitchen tools that belonged to family members—such as a grandparent's rolling pin or a family skillet—as a way of connecting to their energy and love.

The Magic of Cooking Together

Collaborative cooking rituals transform food preparation into an opportunity for connection, healing, and shared magic. Whether it's a comforting meal for a grieving friend, a festive birthday dinner, or a gathering to make preserves, cooking together nurtures both body and spirit.

Each collaborative cooking ritual brings people closer, reinforcing bonds and building a supportive community. By infusing meals with intention, respect, and love, you create a space where everyone feels valued and connected, reminding us that food is far more than sustenance—it is a symbol of love, tradition, and shared magic.

Part 4

Recipes

Recipes

The following are simple recipes you could adopt or adapt in your cooking rituals.

In addition to the ingredients and steps consider what affirmations you may want to add, what dishes you could serve them in, and other magical actions to help build out your unique spell crafting.

Since these are simple recipes they are also perfect for swapping ingredients and intuitive cooking.

SMOOTHIE
RECIPES

Abundance & Grounding

Kick off your day with a boost of vitality and essential nutrients courtesy of this delightful green smoothie!

Ingredients:

- 1/2 avocado (abundance)
- 1/2 banana (joy)
- 1/2 c spinach (healing)
- 1/2 c almond milk (connection)
- 1/2 tbsp honey (harmony)
- A few ice cubes

Place the avocado, banana, spinach, and almond milk in a blender. Add the honey and ice if desired, then blend untili smooth.

Pour into a glass, hold your intention for abundance and grounding. Enjoy.

LOVE AND HEART HEALING SMOOTHIE

This vibrant pink smoothie is designed to foster love, self-compassion, and emotional healing. With strawberries, raspberries, and a hint of vanilla, it's a sweet, romantic blend that nurtures the heart.

INGREDIENTS:

- 1/2 c strawberries (love, passion, and sweetness)
- 1/4c raspberries (healing, intuition, and protection)
- 1/2 c coconut milk (purity, nourishment, and emotional soothing)
- 1/2 tsp vanilla extract (love and mental clarity)
- 1 tsp honey (harmony and connection)

DIRECTIONS:

- Add all ingredients into a blender and blend until smooth.
- Take a moment to focus on feelings of love and healing.
- ENJOY!

"I am worthy of love, and I open my heart to healing and joy. With each breath, I release past hurt and welcome compassion, peace, and self-love into my life."

Energizing & Creativity

SMOOTHIE

Ingredients :

- 1/2 c mango (joy, optimism, and attraction)
- 1/4 c shredded carrots (success, luck, fertility of ideas)
- 1/2 tsp fresh ginger (strength, motivation, and protection)
- 1/2 c orange juice (creativity, happiness, energy)
- a few ice cubes

Directions

- Add ingredients to a blender and blend until smooth.
- Set your intention for creative energy and inspiration.

Salads

Prosperity
PASTA SALAD
ABUNDANCE SUCCESS & GROWTH

- 1 c cooked penne ((movement & progress)
- 1/2 c cherry tomatoes, halved (love & harmony)
- 1/4 c Kalamata olives, sliced (grounding & protection)
- 1/2 c diced cucumber (balance & vitality)
- 1/4 c fresh basil leaves, torn (wealth & abundance)
- 1/4 c feta cheese, crumbled (nourishment & harmony)
- 2 tbsp extra virgin olive oil (healing & unity)
- 1 tbsp balsamic vinegar
- salt & pepper

Combine all ingredients in a medium bowl, toss to combine and distribute

POTATO SALAD

Combine the Following in a Large Bowl

- 2 c boiled and diced potatoes (grounding and protection)
- 1/4 c celery, chopped (balance and clarity)
- 1/4 c diced red onion (courage and strength)
- 2 tbsp fresh dill, chopped (protection and cleansing)
- 2 tbsp fresh parsley, chopped (healing and vitality)
- 1/4 c mayonnaise (comfort and emotional nourishment)
- 1 tbsp Dijon mustard (strength and empowerment)
- Salt and Pepper to taste

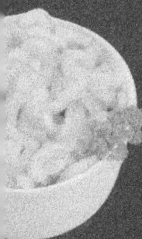

Joyful FRUIT SALAD

This bright, colourful fruit salad is packed with ingredients to elevate joy and happiness. Strawberries bring love, oranges uplift, and blueberries promote calm and peace. This salad is perfect for gatherings or anytime you want to add a little extra joy to your day.

- 1/2 cup strawberries, sliced (love and sweetness)
- 1/2 cup blueberries (calm and peace)
- 1/2 cup pineapple chunks (positivity and abundance)
- 1/2 orange, segmented (creativity and happiness)
- 1 kiwi, peeled and sliced (emotional balance and healing)
- 1 tablespoon honey (harmony and attraction)
- Fresh mint leaves for garnish (clarity and freshness)

SIDE DISHES

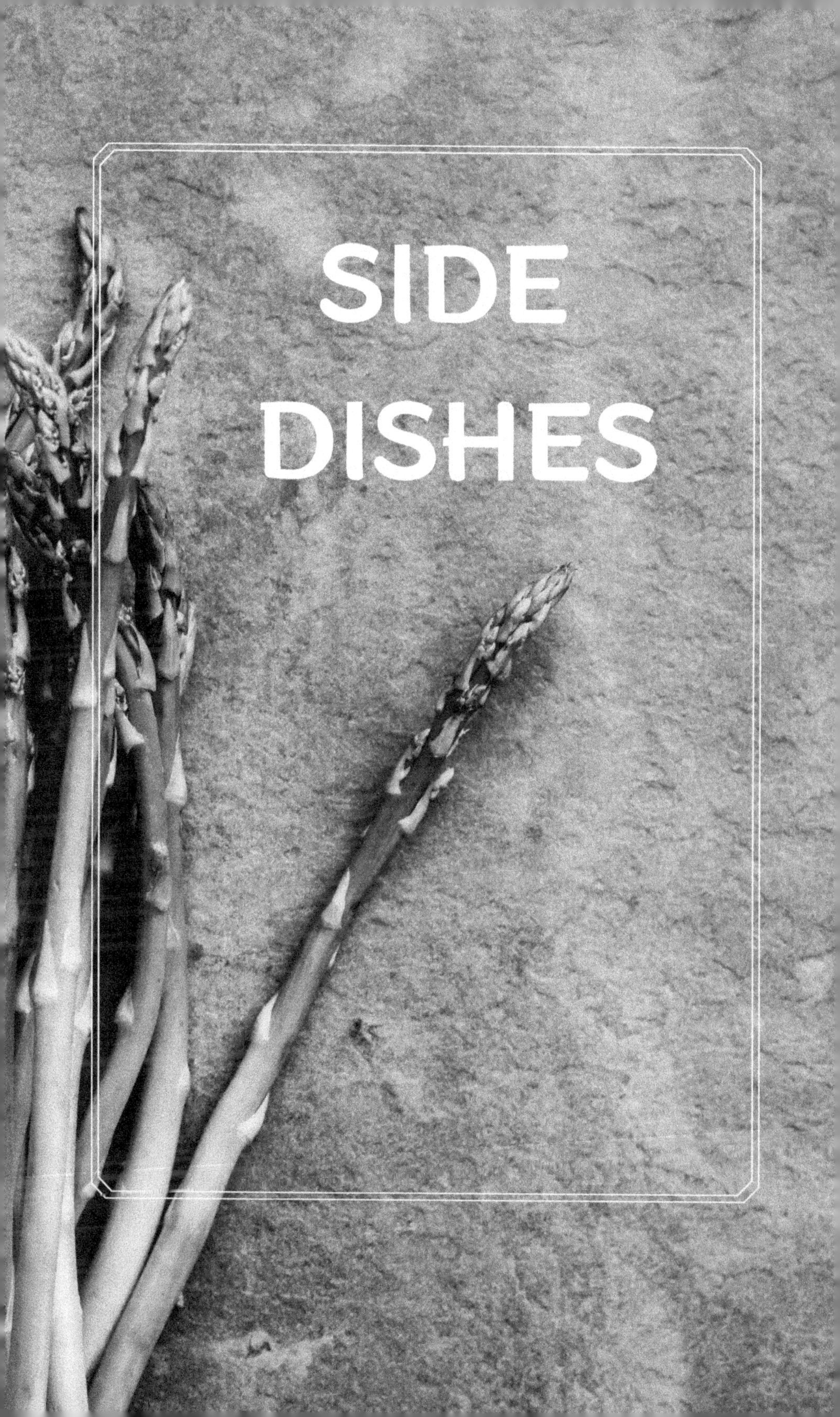

Magical Macaroni & Cheese

T his comforting mac and cheese recipe infuses each ingredient with magical intention, transforming a favorite classic into a nourishing dish for the soul. Each component brings its own energy, making it more than just a meal—it's a spell of warmth, grounding, and abundance. I have been doing this recipe for over twenty years now, and mostly I cook it intuitively, I have added notes on the steps to help identify how the ingredients are changing.

Ingredients

- **4 cups uncooked macaroni (Cavatappi or Scoobi Doos)**: Abundance and growth. The spiraled shape of Cavatappi captures the energy of cycles and renewal, inviting abundance and sustenance into the meal.

- **4 tablespoons butter**: Comfort, unity, and love. Butter adds richness and warmth, symbolizing the nurturing support of self-care and connection.

- **4 tablespoons flour**: Grounding and stability. Flour represents the foundational energy of the earth, grounding the dish and bringing strength.

- **4 cups milk**: Nourishment and emotional harmony. Milk is a symbol of nurturing and comfort, fostering emotional connection and well-being.

- **4 cups shredded old cheddar cheese**: Joy and indulgence. Cheese brings a sense of joy and satisfaction, infusing the dish with warmth, richness, and a touch of celebration. As you experiment, feel free to mix up the cheeses with different blends.

- **1 teaspoon mustard powder**: Clarity and protection. Mustard powder adds a subtle spice that clears away negativity, focusing the energy of the dish on clarity and resilience.

- **1 teaspoon salt**: Purification and balance. Salt purifies and enhances, balancing flavors while amplifying the magical intention.

- **1/2 teaspoon black pepper**: Protection and courage. Black pepper adds a touch of heat, offering protection and empowering the dish with bold energy.

Topping

- **1 tablespoon butter**: Comfort and love. Softens the breadcrumbs, binding the ingredients together with warmth and support.

- **1/4 to 1/3 cup breadcrumbs**: Abundance and grounding. Breadcrumbs represent resources and resilience, reminding us of abundance in even the simplest ingredients.

Instructions

1. Preheat the oven to 375°F (190°C), setting the intention to create a warm, comforting space.

2. Cook the pasta according to package instructions. As it boils, visualize abundance and growth filling the spiraled shapes, ready to bring grounding and sustenance.

3. Prepare the roux: In a medium to large pot, melt the butter on medium heat. Let it turn golden (1-2 minutes), infusing the dish with comfort and unity. Stir in the flour, letting it cook until it emits a nutty aroma, grounding the base of the dish with stability (1-2 minutes).

4. Add the milk gradually, about 1/4 cup at a time, fully incorporating before adding more. Visualize each pour blending harmony and emotional nourishment into the sauce.

5. Thicken the sauce: Continue stirring on medium heat for 7–10 minutes until the sauce is thickened, coating the spoon and holding its shape momentarily. Make sure to be stirring making contact with the bottom

of the pot so it doesn't stick and scorch.

6. Add the cheese: Stir until melted, focusing on the joy, warmth, and indulgence it brings. Blend in the mustard powder, salt, and pepper, visualizing clarity, balance, and protection.

7. Assemble the dish: In a greased 9x11 casserole dish, spread the cooked pasta. Ladle the cheese sauce over it, allowing each layer to settle with the intention of grounding and comfort.

8. Prepare the topping: In a small bowl, blend the butter into the breadcrumbs, imbuing the mixture with unity and abundance. Sprinkle it evenly over the dish.

9. Bake for 30–35 minutes, until the dish is bubbly and golden. Visualize the energy of warmth, nourishment, and comfort coming together in perfect harmony.

10. Let it set: Remove from the oven and let it rest for 5 minutes, allowing the flavors and energies to meld.

11. Enjoy this magical macaroni and cheese, bringing grounding, joy, and comfort with every bite.

Lemon Honey Asparagus

INGREDIENTS

- 1 lb fresh or frozen asparagus trimmed (vitality and renewal)
- 1 tbsp olive oil (healing and unity)
- Zest and juice of 1 lemon (joy and cleansing)
- 1 tbsp honey (love and sweetness)
- Salt and pepper to taste

Intention: Freshness, renewal, and light energy
This zesty asparagus dish brings clarity and cleansing energy, perfect for welcoming in new beginnings.

DIRECTIONS

1. Preheat Oven: Preheat to 400°F (200°C).
2. Prepare Asparagus: Toss the asparagus with olive oil, lemon zest, and juice, and drizzle with honey. Season with salt and pepper, visualizing renewal and light energy filling the dish.
3. Roast: Spread on a baking sheet and roast for 12–15 minutes, until tender.
4. Serve: Savor each bite, embracing the energy of fresh beginnings and vitality.

Stuffed Bell Peppers

Ingridients :

4 large bell peppers, tops cut off and seeds removed (creativity and joy whole vegetable integrity and protection)

1 c cooked quinoa or rice (abundance and sustenance)

1 can (15oz) black beans, drained and rinsed (grounding and resilience)

1/2 c diced onion (clarity and courage)

1/2 c diced tomatoes (love and vitality)

1 tsp cumin (warmth and protection)

1 tsp salt (protection)

1/4 tsp black pepper (protection)

1/4 c chopped cilanto, plus extra for garnish (healing and fresh energy)

1/2 c shredded cheese (optional for harmony and comfort)

Directions :

1. Preheat the Oven: Preheat your oven to 375°F (190°C).
2. Prepare the Filling: In a large bowl, combine the cooked quinoa or rice, black beans, diced onion, diced tomatoes, cumin, salt, black pepper, and chopped cilantro. Stir well, focusing on abundance, prosperity, and joy as you mix.
3. Stuff the Peppers: Fill each bell pepper with the mixture, packing it in to ensure each pepper is full. If desired, sprinkle a bit of shredded cheese on top for added comfort and harmony.
4. Bake: Arrange the stuffed peppers upright in a baking dish, adding a small amount of water to the bottom of the dish to help steam the peppers. Cover the dish with foil and bake for 25 minutes. Remove the foil and bake for an additional 10–15 minutes, or until the peppers are tender and the filling is heated through.
5. Garnish and Serve: Garnish with extra cilantro and enjoy, focusing on the energy of abundance and joy with each bite

Mushroom Risotto

Ingridients :

2 tbsp olive oil
1 small chopped onion
2 c mushrooms sliced
1 garlic clove minced
1 c Arborio rice
1/2 c white wine

4 c vegetable broth (warmed)
1 tbsp fresh thyme
sale and pepper to taste
1/4 c grated Parmesan cheese
Fresh parsley for garnish

WISDOM AND INTUITION

Directions :

1. Keep the broth warm in a saucepan on the stovetop.
2. Heat the olive oil over medium heat in a large skillet or saucepan. Add the onion and cook until translucent, about 3 minutes. Add the mushrooms and garlic, cooking until they release their moisture and are golden (5-7 mins.)
3. Stir in the Arborio rice, coating it with the oil and aromatics for about 1-2 minutes.
4. Pour in the white wine (if using), stirring until the liquid is mostly absorbed. Begin adding the warm broth one ladleful at a time, stirring frequently and allowing each addition to be mostly absorbed before adding the next. Continue for about 18-20 minutes, until the rice is creamy and tender.
5. Stir in the thyme, salt, pepper, and Parmesan
6. Garnish with fresh parsley and enjoy.

Green Beans
With Slivered Almonds

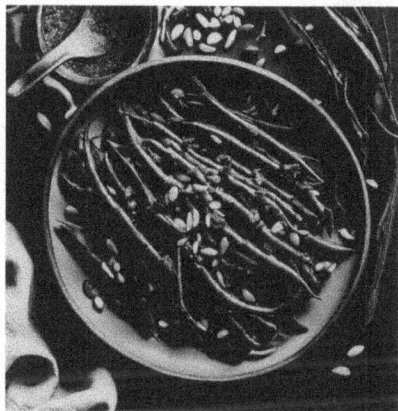

**INTENTION:
ABUNDANCE,
RESILIENCE, AND
PROTECTION**

Made 3 Ways

Fresh

Frozen

Canned

Magical Green Beans with Slivered Almonds for Prosperity and Resilience

Intention: Abundance, resilience, and protection

This green bean side dish is adaptable to fresh, frozen, or canned beans and adds a touch of warmth with spices for prosperity and balance.

Ingredients:

1 lb green beans, trimmed (if fresh) or 2 cans (14.5 oz each) or 1 lb frozen (prosperity and growth)

1 tablespoon olive oil or butter (healing and unity)

1/3 cup slivered almonds (protection and resilience)

1/2 teaspoon garlic powder (protection)

1/2 teaspoon smoked paprika (warmth and abundance)

Salt and pepper to taste (balance and harmony)

Instructions:

Prepare the Green Beans:

- Fresh Beans: Steam or boil fresh beans until just tender, about 5–7 minutes, then drain.

- Frozen Beans: Thaw by steaming or microwaving, then drain excess water.

- Canned Beans: Drain and rinse the beans.

Toast the Almonds: In a large skillet over medium heat, add the slivered almonds. Toast for 2–3 minutes, stirring frequently until golden brown. Remove from skillet and set aside.

Sauté the Green Beans: In the same skillet, heat olive oil or butter over medium heat. Add the green beans, stirring to coat. Add garlic powder and smoked paprika, focusing on the intentions of protection and abundance as you stir.

Season and Serve: Add salt and pepper to taste, tossing until beans are heated through and coated in the spices. Sprinkle with toasted almonds and serve.

Each bite brings the grounding energy of the earth, the resilience of almonds, and the warming spices, helping you feel connected to prosperity and harmony with each serving.

DESSERTS

APPLE CRISP

INGREDIENTS:

- 4 apples, peeled and sliced (health and love)
- 1/2 cup brown sugar (joy and grounding)
- 1 teaspoon cinnamon (protection and warmth)
- 1/2 cup flour (stability and grounding)
- 1/2 cup oats (abundance and resilience)
- 1/3 cup butter, melted (comfort and unity)

INSTRUCTIONS

- Preheat Oven: Set the oven to 350°F (175°C).
- Prepare Apple Base: In a bowl, toss the apple slices with cinnamon and a bit of brown sugar, focusing on gratitude for each ingredient.
- Make the Topping: Mix flour, oats, remaining brown sugar, and melted butter, setting an intention for grounding and warmth.
- Bake: Place apples in a baking dish and sprinkle the topping evenly over them. Bake for 30–35 minutes, until golden and bubbling.
- Serve: Enjoy this comforting dish, savoring each bite with a focus on gratitude and appreciation.

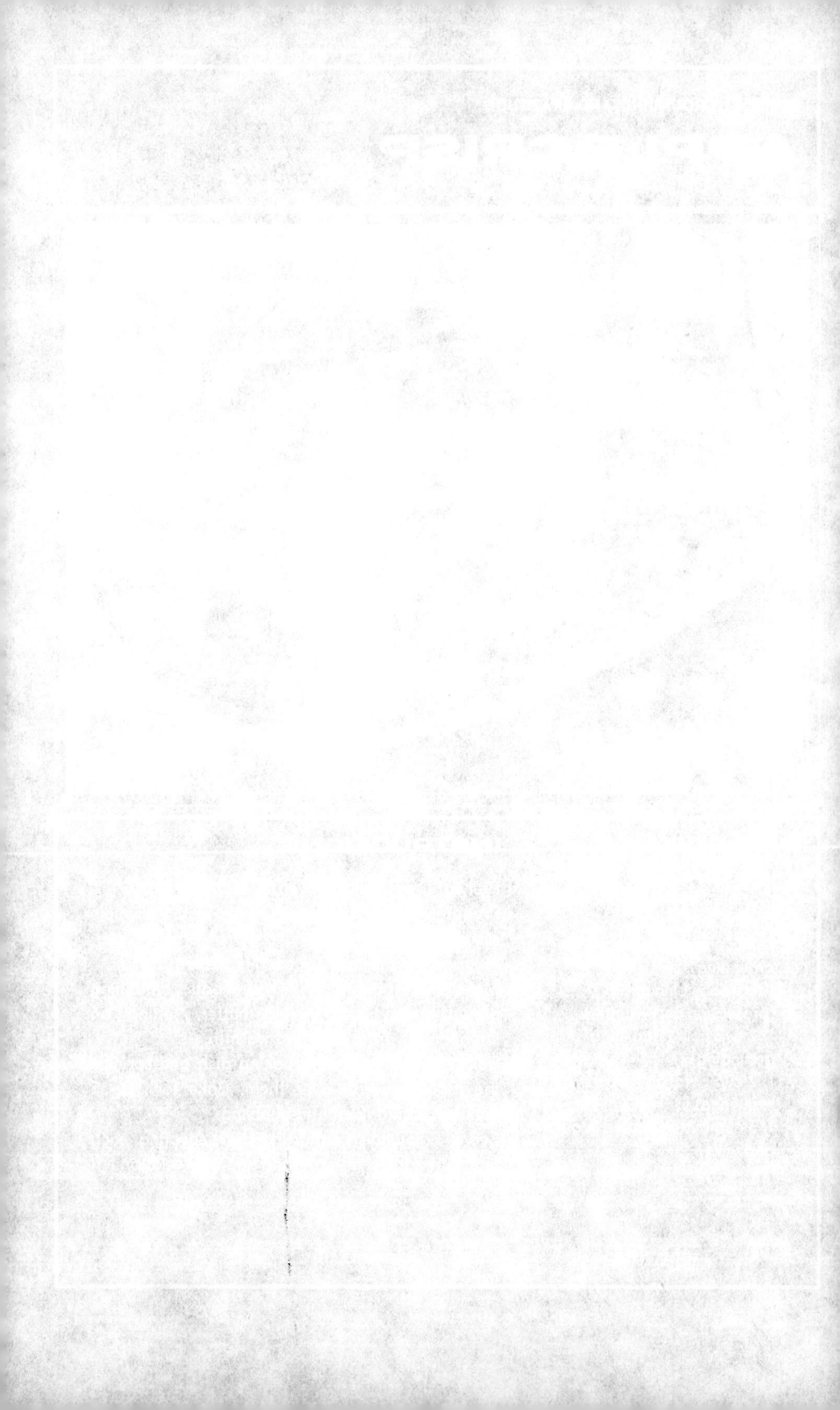

CINNAMON HONEY SHORTBREAD COOKIES
for Warmth and Comfort

Ingridients :

- 1 cup butter, softened (comfort and unity)
- 1/2 cup powdered sugar (joy and lightness)
- 2 cups flour (abundance and grounding)
- 1 tablespoon honey (love and sweetness)
- 1 teaspoon cinnamon (warmth and protection)

Directions :

1. Cream Butter and Sugar: In a bowl, beat the butter and powdered sugar until light and fluffy. Stir in honey, focusing on love and comfort.
2. Add Flour and Cinnamon: Mix in the flour and cinnamon, visualizing warmth and grounding energy infusing the dough.
3. Shape and Chill: Form the dough into a log, wrap it in plastic, and chill for 30 minutes.
4. Bake: Preheat the oven to 350°F (175°C). Slice the dough into rounds, add a few pokes, and place on a baking sheet. Bake for 10–12 minutes, until edges are golden. Let the comforting aroma fill the kitchen as they bake.
5. Serve: Enjoy each cookie as a moment of harmony and self-love, embracing the soothing warmth.

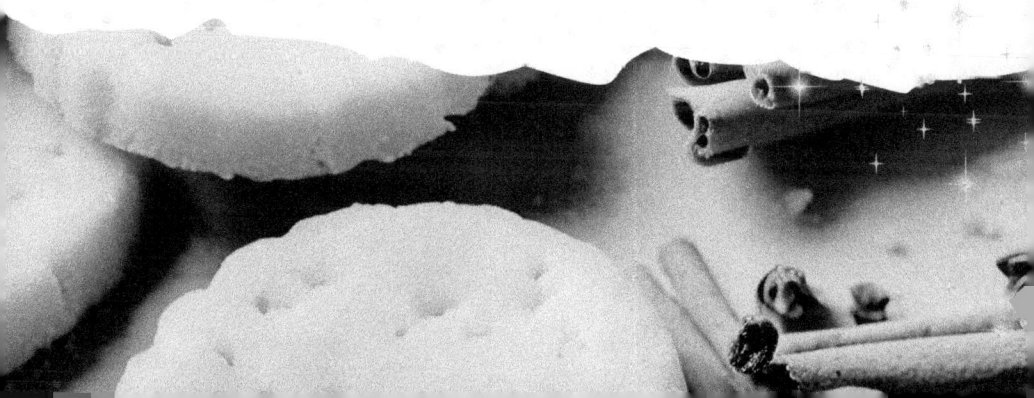

Choco-Avocado Mousse

LOVE & SELF-WORTH

Ingredients:

- 2 ripe avocados (self-love and new beginnings)
- 1/4 cup cocoa powder (love and passion)
- 1/4 cup honey or maple syrup (sweetness and joy)
- 1/4 cup almond milk (nurturing and comfort)
- 1 teaspoon vanilla extract (clarity and warmth)

Steps for Cooking:

1. Blend Ingredients: Combine avocados, cocoa powder, honey, almond milk, and vanilla in a food processor. Blend until smooth, visualizing self-love and empowerment filling the mixture.

2. Chill and Serve: Spoon the mousse into bowls and chill for 30 minutes. Serve as a nourishing, rich dessert, embracing self-worth and inner warmth.

Thank you

Thank You for Reading!

Thank you for joining me on this journey—I'm so grateful for your time and support! Your feedback means a lot to me, and hearing from readers is one of the best parts of being an author. If you enjoyed the book, I'd love it if you could take a moment to share your thoughts in a review on Amazon. Your reviews help other readers discover my work, and I appreciate every word.

If you'd like to reach out directly, feel free to contact me at Kelsey.Pearce.Grit@gmail.com. I'd be delighted to hear from you!

With heartfelt thanks,

Kelsey

Also by Kelsey Pearce

Mindful Magic Series:

Mindful Magic: A Guide to Modern Witchcraft for Mental Wellness & Self-Care   ISBN 978-1738290574

A beginners guide to magic and intention. This book takes a inclusive and accessible approach to magic encouraging anyone to build their our practice. Learn how to create your own spells or leverage the twenty-five premade spells.

Mindful Magic for The Holiday Witch: A Guide to Winter Solstice, Yule Rituals, Self-Care, and Holiday Healing ISBN 978-1069149114

Transformative approach to the holiday season. Drawing on the timeless magic of Yule and witchcraft traditions, this guide empowers you to create a more meaningful, grounded, and balanced holiday experience.

Mindful Magic for The Work Witch: Integrating Witchcraft and Self-Care in the Professional Realm ISBN 978-1069149121

Drawing on universal concepts of mindfulness and magic, this book helps you unlock tools for intention-setting, energy management, and growth, all while staying grounded in the practical demands of the modern workplace.

Spell Crafting: Witchcraft resource that includes reference material for crystals, herbs, lunar magic, and more. ISBN 978-1738290567

Build your own Book of Shadows or Grimoire with these easy templates and reference material.

Resiliency and Gratitude Series:

Grateful Grit: Building Resilience Through Gratitude   ISBN 978-1738290529

Learn how gratitude in the face of adversity can help build resilience and your growth mindset.

Happiness for the Senses: Mindful Sensory Experience: Taste, Touch, Sight, Smell, Sound ISBN 978-1738290505

Learn how to engage all of your senses to find happiness and mindfulness.